Praise for *Hope in Sight*

"Riveting! Dr. Simjee, an ophthalmologist par excellence, is a superb storyteller. Each chapter of *Hope in Sight* reads like an adventure, filled with powerful moments of courage and compassion."

—*Manoj Kulkarni, MD, Director of Preoperative Assessment,*
Allied Anesthesia Medical Group

"I am hopeful that after reading this journal younger ophthalmologists will be inspired to perform missionary trips to third-world countries and perform similar surgeries to restore vision from blindness. It is a wonderful account from a true humanitarian."

—*Roger V. Ohanesian, MD, ophthalmologist and founder,*
Armenian EyeCare Project

"Dr. Simjee's life exemplifies what a diminutive woman with a large heart and force of will can do to restore the vision of many and enhance the humanity in all of us."

—*Lytton W. Smith, MD, FAAFP, CMD, Past President,*
Orange County Medical Association, and former Chief of Staff,
St. Jude Medical Center

"This book should be read by the entire medical profession: students, interns, residents, nurses, and practicing physicians. It will inspire and motivate them to volunteer for medical missions, and it will endow them with a purpose-driven life."

—*Carl Lum, MD, Mission Director, Aloha Medical Mission*

"Dr. Simjee's book is a testament to how much of a difference one person can make in the

—*Julie Holt* h Health System

"*Hope in Sight* is an amazing journey.... Small in stature yet generous and courageous of heart, Dr. Simjee demonstrates compassion that reaches out and encompasses the world."
—*Sister Charleen Robinson, CSJ, Sisters of St. Joseph of Orange*

"As an immigrant to the United States and as a woman physician, I can relate to Dr. Simjee's love for this country and for the practice of medicine, which clearly shines through the text of her book. "
—*Maria E. Minon, MD, Vice President Medical Affairs and Chief Medical Officer, CHOC Children's*

"An engaging account of an enlightening journey with the power to move readers deeply."
—*Sam Achs, MD, general surgeon*

"*Hope in Sight* allows us to see the most underserved world through the 20/20 vision of a real foot soldier and a dedicated humanitarian— a wonderful piece of work."
—*Sudeep Kukreja, MD, founder, Arpan Global Charities*

"An inspirational journey of paying it forward! Dr. Simjee's stories provide vision into her personal struggles, triumphs, and life experiences of restoring sight and dignity that renew humanity and motivate us to appraise what legacy we will leave behind."
—*Wendy Ferro-Grant, RN, BSN, CNOR, Clinical Manager, St. Joseph Hospital Outpatient Surgery Center*

"Dr. Simjee takes the reader into a world most of us never see. Each chapter reads like an adventure story. But at its heart, the book is about service and passion and commitment. It speaks to the impact that a dedicated physician has had on the lives of people born into unimaginable poverty. And while the focus is always on those in need, it cannot help but be a tribute to a remarkable woman."
—*Linda Simon, Vice President, Mission Integration, St. Joseph Hospital*

"It is a great book on a fantastic woman of the world."
—*Ellena M. Peterson, PhD, Professor, Department of Pathology;*
Associate Dean, Admissions and Outreach;
and Associate Director, Medical Microbiology,
School of Medicine, University of California, Irvine

"*Hope in Sight* is a touching and inspiring tale, a must-read for anyone interested in making an impact on the world. I found great motivation in Dr. Simjee's vision for creating a better world, one eye at a time. Having been on three medical missions with her, I admire her level of energy, enthusiasm, and flexibility for operating in the worst of conditions. I continue to be humbled by her dedication to her patients and her passion for service, locally and abroad. An absolute inspiration!"
—*Bishoy Said, MD, ophthalmologist in training,*
University of California, Irvine, School of Medicine

"It is truly inspirational to read about Dr. Simjee's journey from Burma to California and how she risked everything she had in order to help those people she will most likely never see again—but they will."
—*Doug Katsev, MD, ophthalmologist*

"Dr. Simjee's humble accounts of providing for others transcend human kindness and compassion and inspire others to following her footsteps."
—*Betsy Dilsisian, RN, BSN, CNOR, Operations Manager,*
St. Joseph Hospital Outpatient Surgery Center

"I am reminded of what Lord Buddha said: 'Fashion your life as a garland of beautiful deeds.' That is what Aisha has done and, I am sure, will continue doing for the rest of her life."
—*Win May, MD, PhD, Professor and Director, Clinical Skills*
Education and Evaluation Center, Division of Medical Education,
Keck School of Medicine, University of Southern California

"Dr. Simjee has reinstated my belief that there are really good people in this world. Powerful stories. Powerful woman."

—Emily Guichet, California Community Leader

"As the former CEO of an agency that has had the pleasure of hosting Dr. Aisha Simjee twice on the ground—first in Haiti and then again in Pakistan—I can personally attest to her grit, determination, generous heart, attention to detail, and, above all, supreme care and attention for her patients. She stands out among all the doctors we have deployed as someone who has demonstrated true humility in the service of the underprivileged, and she will never, ever give up or admit defeat against even the most difficult odds. She exudes energy and positivism and is an inspiration for all of us who work in public service."

—Laila Karamally, Executive Director,
Developments in Literacy, and Former CEO, SHINE Humanity

"No area of the world is too remote, no condition too primitive, no facility too meager, to keep Dr. Simjee from performing surgeries and treating patients who need her special skills. In *Hope in Sight*, Dr. Simjee tells her amazing life story, but her greatest hope is that it will inspire others to reach out to help those in need—wherever they are in our world."

—Marcia Cooley, Assistant Professor (Ret.),
English Language Institute, Chapman University

"What an incredible accomplishment from a difficult set of life circumstances. Her dedication to helping others is outstanding and truly moves one to also help others who are not able to help themselves."

—Richard S. Fields, MD, JD

"I have been so enthralled by Dr. Simjee's story. And so inspired and informed. It is jam-packed with history, technology, altruism, loyalty, compassion, and courage. I would encourage anyone to experience Dr. Simjee through this book."

—Sali Fox Edwards, Library Media Specialist

"*Hope in Sight* is a great description of the journey of Dr. Simjee's life... This book should serve as a great inspiration for anyone wanting to undertake global medical missions to tackle the worldwide eye crisis."
—*Satinder Swaroop, MD, FACO, FACC, Clinical Professor, University of California, Irvine, School of Medicine*

"In *Hope in Sight*, Aisha Simjee, MD, takes us on her journey to bring renewed sight to many parts of the world where poverty and political situations prevent the most basic medical care. This good book is not a romance story. It is about truth and dedication. It is about living in different parts of the world and being a participating citizen of that world. It is about reality. It will cause you to question your service to mankind."
—*Chris Layton, Past Chair, St. Joseph Hospital Foundation*

"Dr. Simjee has written an important book about her life as an ophthalmologist delivering medical and surgical care to the hopeless blind in the third world. This well-written, fascinating book is a must-read for anyone who is involved in, or wants to become involved in, treating surgically curable blindness in the third world."
—*John Crowder, MD, Medical Director, Surgical Eye Expeditions International*

"Dr. Simjee's book details how she spans the globe to prevent blindness, cure the sightless, and teach others healing techniques. She channels *The Little Engine That Could* meets the Energizer Bunny and Mother Teresa meets Mma Ramotswe."
—*Dana M. Holliday, cofounder, SOLO Eyewear*

"Dr. Simjee's stories and experiences have a way of connecting us all to many of the events in our lifetime, such as 9/11 and the Night Stalker, and to the lives of people across the globe. And hers is not a finished story."
—*Steven C. Moreau, President and CEO, St. Joseph Hospital*

"Dr. Simjee's life story inspires and calls all of us to count our blessings and to make each and every day of our lives count."
—*Lou Correa, State Senator, 34th District, California*

Hope in Sight

*One Doctor's Quest
to Restore Eyesight and Dignity
to the World's Poor*

AISHA SIMJEE, MD

WHITE SPRUCE PRESS
ORANGE, CALIFORNIA

White Spruce Press
655 S. Main Street, #310
Orange, CA 92868

Ordering Information
Orders by US trade bookstores and wholesalers. Please contact Independent Publishers Group: Tel. (800) 888-IPG1; Fax. (312) 337-5985, Online, orders@ipgbook .com; or write to Independent Publishers Group, Order Department, 814 North Franklin Street, Chicago, IL 60610.

Quantity sales. Special discounts are available on quantity purchases by corporations, associations, and others. For details, contact the "Special Sales Department" at the address above.

Printed in the United States of America

Cataloging-in-Publication

Simjee, Aisha.
    Hope in sight : one doctor's quest to restore eyesight and dignity to the world's poor / Aisha Simjee.
        p. cm.
    Includes bibliographical references and index.
    ISBN 978-0-9857664-3-6 (pbk)

    1. Simjee, Aisha. 2. Ophthalmologists—Biography. 3. Eye—Diseases.
4. People with visual disabilities—Services for. 5. Poor—Medical care.
I. Title.
    RE36.S56H67 2012   617.7'092
    QBI12-600212

First Edition
17 16 15 14 13   10 9 8 7 6 5 4 3 2 1

Copyediting: PeopleSpeak
Cover Design: Peri Poloni-Gabriel, Knockout Design
Interior Design: Graffolio

617.7
SIM

*Dedicated to people with poor vision
around the world.*

Contents

Preface

Whatever you do, do it with full commitment.
That is the secret for a gratifying life.

AISHA SIMJEE, MD

Why am I sharing my life story? The short answer is that it can be an encouragement to anyone who wants to live a more productive and meaningful life, even under the most undesirable circumstances.

I have been blessed in myriad ways, and my time has been filled with adventures, heartaches, and triumphs. Yet as none of the women in my family have lived past the age of seventy-five, as that number draws closer for me, I awake every day with an urgency to impart what I have seen and learned.

My life's work involves peering into the eyes and souls of my patients to understand what they are feeling and experiencing. However, sharing my personal feelings and experiences, which I've recorded in a stack of diaries since my days as a student in Burma and throughout my medical missions, presented a new challenge for me.

Many friends, family members, colleagues, and patients have spurred me to write this book, sharing experiences from seven decades and insights learned as a Simjee, an Asian immigrant, a mother, a member of a Muslim family, and an ophthalmic surgeon working to improve patients' sight in the far corners of the earth. Their encouragement caused me to consider: *Could the telling of my encounters help bring focus to global health challenges? Might I spark someone's interest in eye health missions and other people-empowering outreach?*

My story is full of adventure but not embellished with romantic tales. More often than not, time constraints on mission trips prevented me from knowing how my interventions changed the course of patients' lives, an aspect of my practice that I enjoy immensely back home in Orange County, California.

According to the World Health Organization (WHO), three-quarters of all blindness can be prevented or treated. Worldwide, about 285 million people are visually impaired due to various causes, and 39 million of them are blind. About 90 percent of the visually impaired live in developing countries.[1] Cataracts (a clouding of the lens of the eye that blocks the passage of light) rank as the leading cause of blindness, except in the more developed countries.[2] In the United States, cataract removal surgery has become one of the most common, safe, and effective operations performed. According to the National Institutes of Health, in at least 90 percent of cases, people who have cataract surgery have better vision afterward.[3]

Eye care should be a key component of the development agendas for struggling nations and communities. The needs are overwhelming. Projections are that by 2020, there will be *76 million blind people* in our world.[4] Seeing so many blind and starving people, I sometimes have to struggle to repress my tears. I know my emotion won't help them. Instead, doing what I can for someone with what is available gives expression to my inner turmoil.

Restoring to those in poverty the dignity, independence, and productivity that comes with sight is profoundly satisfying, and there are plenty of opportunities. The need is so great that sometimes I imagine myself standing in a field with a banner reading "SOS" (Save Our Sight). Many outstanding people and organizations are responding to our global eye crisis, including some introduced in this book. Our world needs many more.

What I've been able to accomplish is only a "drop in the bucket." Yet for a man who was able to return to work, a woman who simply wanted to cook and care for her family, and a child whose dismal prospects were opened through eye care, I had the privilege of changing the course of their lives.

For you, dear reader, I recount the experiences of a no-nonsense scientist and surgeon who believes each of us has the power to transform lives, including our own. *Just by purchasing this book you are empowering eye care, since profits will be used used for future mission trips I take or given to charitable organizations I have worked with that are dedicated to restoring sight to the blind and visually impaired.*

Anyone considering global mission expeditions needs to be prepared to withstand the sacrifices and hardships inherent in most humanitarian missions. It takes more than a passing desire. Volunteers motivated by ego gratification may not have the mental and physical fortitude to withstand shivering in the bitingly cold air of a flood victim camp in north Pakistan; sweating in a hot, humid refugee camp for Haitian earthquake survivors; or laboring at a 12,800-foot altitude serving the native Indians in the mountains of Peru. While I take every precaution I can, my affairs are always in order before I leave on a mission trip, just in case I don't survive it.

For those who can commit to the rigors of service, at home or abroad, a life of depth, significance, and adventure awaits.

Acknowledgments

As English is my fifth language and I have a very heavy work schedule, it was crucial that I have a reliable writer to assist me with this project. I am pleased to have found Sheila Holliday and especially appreciate her willingness to correspond and follow up even while I was overseas. I cannot thank her enough.

1
Burma

My top priority is for people to understand that they have the power to change things themselves.
AUNG SAN SUU KYI

My mother never made it past the second grade, and my father never went to school. So how was I able to become the first woman in my Indian Burmese tribe to graduate from high school, the first to go to college, the first to become a doctor, and the first to come to the United States? None of these achievements came easily, but then realizing one's dreams is rarely easy.

Patience, I used to remind myself when my path seemed overwhelming or I became frustrated navigating my country's political hotbed. When social barriers blocked my ambitions, with quiet determination I risked shaming my family and myself by pursuing a completely different life from the one expected of me. *I will not let the fact that I am a woman stop me*, I vowed.

While I tested my family's deeply embedded traditional values, my respect never wavered. I cherish my forefathers' legacy of drive, dedication, generosity, and triumph in the face of adversity. For Indians, the tribal society we are born into represents more than a geographic commonality. We are bound together by our history, religion, politics, and communal interdependence.

Long before I was born, Great-Grandfather Simjee was an ambitious silk merchant in Gujarat, a state in Western India. The area chief would not allow him the freedom to reach out for better business opportunities, so in 1860 he left India by ship and settled in Burma, the landmass between India and China, in what was then the capital city of Yangon, which ironically can be translated as "end of strife." Under British occupation, the city became known as Rangoon. Eventually he settled in Pyay Myo, also called Prome, about 180 miles northwest of Yangon. Like *Rangoon* versus *Yangon*, *Burma* was easier for Westerners to pronounce than *Myanmar*, which has since been reclaimed as the country's official name.

Great-Grandfather Simjee became a successful merchant of chinaware, and he opened multiple stores. He was also a philanthropist, opening small schools and a mosque. He built simple, thatched-roof garden huts where his employees could live, creating a neighborhood known as Simjee Chaan, which still exists. The family business, Simjee & Sons, was passed down to my grandfather and then to my uncles and my father, Yoosuf, who further expanded the family business.

My mother, Amina, came from Mauritius, a small island in the Indian Ocean near Madagascar, off the southeast coast of Africa, where her family farmed sugar cane. Her mother died when she was eight years old, and her father moved the family to Surat, India, so that his relatives could help raise her and seven siblings. In 1932, Amina wed my father through an arranged marriage, and Yoosuf took his new bride back to Burma.

Yoosuf and Amina Simjee had four children. I was the youngest, born near the end of World War II. Because of Burma's strategic location, Japanese planes invaded Burma days after the bombing of Pearl Harbor. My family lost nearly everything to the invaders except what gold and rubies they were able to bury in our backyard, underneath the remains of a storage shed that the occupiers had burned. Life became difficult and dangerous for my family. The Japanese made "examples" of leading citizens to intimidate the masses into following their rules. In front of the local market, my father's elder brother was tortured to the point of having his back broken, and he never walked again.

A significant number of the Simjee clan fled the country. They walked back to India, through the region that is now Bangladesh. My father stayed behind to find someone to watch over his property and sent my mother and their first three children, ages eight, six, and two, ahead of him. On their trek of roughly fifteen hundred miles they passed through dense tropical jungles and swamps, risking chance encounters with thieves, tigers, and cobras, vipers, and other venomous snakes proliferating in the area. For the next two and a half months my family and a bullock pulling a cart trudged along to reach India.

A few months later, when my father felt his property was secure in the hands of a trusted employee, he too came to India, practically walking over dead bodies that had succumbed to trauma, disease, and starvation. Our family stayed in the western India city of Surat, which was far less affected by the war, for the next six years. This is where I was born in 1944.

In 1947 Burma gained its independence from the United Kingdom, and by 1951 all of the Simjee clan had returned. Business was booming, and my father grew to be the sixth wealthiest man in the country. His industries included plants for hardware and aluminum production and distribution. He sold his products to the masses at inexpensive prices. His textile mill manufactured blankets sold through a contract with the army and navy.

Rangoon (now Yangon) lies near the convergence of the Yangon and Bago Rivers. I grew up in a large, four-story home that my family built in the center of the bustling, upscale downtown on what was then called Dalhousie Road. I lived with about forty-five Simjee clan members, including my siblings, cousins, and other relatives. Each room had a ceiling fan to cool us in the summers. My brother, sisters, and I shared one of the bedrooms, sleeping on thin cotton mattresses. Because of the hot, humid Burmese climate, we left our doors and windows open. To protect against disease-carrying mosquitoes, each of our beds was draped in a net hung from the ceiling.

When I was seven years of age I contracted trachoma, the world's leading cause of preventable blindness,[1] caused by chlamydia germs. Common in developing countries and rarely seen in the United States, trachoma begins as an inflammation of the tissue lining the eyelids (conjunctivitis or pinkeye) and left untreated can lead to scarring and loss of sight. There had been an outbreak of trachoma among the local schoolchildren. We had no medicines to treat the disease, so as was common practice in our community, my family found a young, nursing mother who would lay me in her lap and squirt breast milk in my eye. Fortunately, this folk remedy worked! The sterile, protein-rich fluid helped heal my eyes. From this experience came my fascination with eye health, and I set my sights on becoming an eye doctor.

Even as a young child I recall thirsting to learn. Some of my earliest memories are of the small, local schools I attended, which had no art or extracurricular activities. In one school I learned two languages: Gujarati, my tribal language, and Urdu, widely spoken in Pakistan and India. I then attended Madrassa Noor Ul Islam, a private primary school where I learned to read Arabic so that I could read the Qur'an. Next, I enrolled in St. John's Convent, where I learned English and the basic tenets of Catholicism—required learning for all its students. After that I attended a small, private Burmese school to complete my high school education.

Neither my brother nor my two sisters completed middle or high school. It was simply not expected. My brother was to stay in my father's shops and help run the business. The girls were raised to stay home and cook, sew, and clean house. Marriages were usually arranged by the time a child was sixteen years of age. My sisters were married at seventeen and nineteen and my brother by the age of twenty-one. My parents arranged a marriage for me as well and were upset when I told them I didn't want to marry. "I want to go to college," I insisted. "If you force me to wed I will run away." Surely they realized as I did that in Burma I had nowhere to run and hide. I'm glad I wasn't the firstborn or even the second daughter, for whom marriage was mandatory, or they never would have accepted my plans.

In 1961, when I was seventeen, my immediate family traveled to Saudi Arabia for the Hajj pilgrimage to Mecca. This was my first trip out of Burma. Because at that time my father was very wealthy, we were able to travel throughout the Middle East for two and a half months. We visited Medina, Saudi Arabia, the second holiest site for Muslims, as well as Jerusalem, another holy destination. Lands of historic and religious significance that I had studied in school came alive for me. I felt fortunate to have up-close views of the Middle East's Dead Sea and major cities in Jordan, Egypt, Syria, and Iraq.

Once home, I continued in the small Burmese high school, where I studied for the local matriculation exam, which was required to attend the local university. I had none of the social distractions that can detract from a teen's studies. My classmates were primarily Burmese and Chinese, with only two other Indian students. Being the only Muslim student, I alone wore a hijab. While I occasionally had friends visit my home, my family would not have approved of me, a girl past puberty, visiting their homes.

I took and passed the exam with honors and was admitted to Rangoon University for premed studies, qualifying for admission to University of Medicine 1, Rangoon. During my first summer at the university, students launched a demonstration against the government. Although I sympathized, I never took part in the demonstrations. I had done enough against my family's wishes and wanted to avoid any trouble. That approach kept me safe.

On July 7, 1962, dozens of demonstrating students—an accurate count was never reported—were massacred, including students I knew.[2] Police and military forces dynamited the Students' Union building. Several of my classmates and I hid in a six-foot gutter until the gunfire subsided. I found and jumped on a bus going downtown and hurriedly walked the rest of the way home. Although shaken, I felt grateful to be unharmed.

While I concentrated on my medical schooling, my country was greatly afflicted under the new socialist regime. The prime minister and entire cabinet were put in prison, and the military seized control of all businesses, including my father's businesses. Even our family cars were taken. Several members of our tribe were also put in prison because the new government was afraid they would incite a revolt. However, the junta was unable to run my family's businesses, so they put my father back in charge of operations and let us stay in our home.

Intermarriages were not an option in my traditional family, and the new government discriminated against people of Indian origin. They didn't like our "entrepreneurial tendencies." My parents used to warn my siblings and me, "Families who have money are likely to be targeted for bribery and harassment. Always be on guard and don't draw attention to yourself."

In spite of the treacherous times, the new dictator, General Ne Win, did not hurt anyone in my immediate family. The general's father and my grandfather had known each other years earlier in Prome. Although Grandfather Simjee was not Buddhist, he had donated a large amount of money for a housing project to help the people living in the area surrounding their temple. Ne Win's father had built the housing project.

Still, our family lived under a shadow, wondering who would be prosecuted next. I was never afraid, but I was very careful not to attract unwanted attention. My parents repeatedly cautioned, "Don't talk about anything with anybody," and I dutifully complied.

By keeping a low profile, I was able to continue my education in spite of the political instability. While in the medical school complex I gave up wearing the hijab. My Burmese classmates had no reason to wear them, and I enjoyed this small freedom. But at the end of the day I would put it on before our housekeeper picked me up and took me home. My tribe would have been outraged, and my family would have lost face in the Islamic community if I had been seen without it.

Throughout my high school and university years, I frequently found my way to the town's local library, one of more than one hundred United States Information Service Libraries built all over Southeast Asia before, during, and after World War II. Many people believed that the purpose of these libraries, some of which still exist today, was to disseminate American propaganda. Others, including myself, considered them places of education, ideas, and democratic access.

I went frequently to read about the Western world. I would devour periodicals such as *Time* magazine—with a dictionary at my elbow. The stories I read of Western women excelling in science and world affairs fanned my desire to be one of those women. Reports on the Equal Pay Act of 1963, requiring equal pay for US men and women performing the same job duties, and Katharine Graham becoming president of the *Washington Post* impressed and intrigued me.

As I read, I became more familiar with the political and cultural landscape of America. But with the military takeover, the library was burned to the ground.

The last time I visited the former site of the library—standing where charred remains replaced what had been for me an oasis of knowledge— was an incredibly depressing day. More than forty years later, I am still saddened when I read about the unjust military regime that has controlled Burma for six decades, resulting in Burmese people being among the most oppressed and impoverished in the world. (Finally, by late 2011, we began to see democratic progress, giving hope that life in Burma will improve.)

After the constant barrage of violence surrounding me in war-torn Burma, I grew numb to my feelings of anger, pain, hurt, and disappointment. It was the only way I could cope with the injustices inflicted upon my countrymen. With more conviction than ever, I made up my mind that I wanted to leave the country and the conflict behind as soon as I graduated. When I told my family they were stunned—speechless—but had no reason to keep me there. I recall the tension in our house, and the disapproval written all over the faces of my older cousins, who felt that my leaving as a single woman would bring shame on the Simjee name and could quite possibly lead to my parents being questioned and harassed.

Before receiving their medical diplomas, students were required to complete a one-year internship. I trained at large government hospitals, such as Rangoon General Hospital; Rangoon Dufferin Hospital, a large maternity center; and Rangoon Children's Hospital. During my training I also cared for patients in leprosy and tuberculosis hospitals outside Rangoon. Then and now, the prevalence rates of leprosy and tuberculosis in Burma rank among the highest in the world.[3]

While at Dufferin, I met an influential Burmese man whose wife was having a baby. I took extra time "bringing them my salt," as we say in my native culture. It means greeting someone with a simple, thoughtful gift, usually of food, to win his or her favor. In this case I was looking after the wife's health, delighting with the couple in their baby's arrival, and bringing them tasty snacks during my visits. I took good care of the wife and delivered her baby. Thank goodness it was a son, as they had daughters and were hoping for a boy.

The woman was happy that I had stayed with her throughout her labor. Talking quietly in the hospital and subsequently during visits to the couple's home, they helped me strategize how to secure my exit papers. The information and ideas they shared about the process for applying to leave Burma proved invaluable. They advised me to keep secret my plans to go to the United States, so that I would not be pressured to pay enormous bribes to officials hoping to cash in on my future income in what they knew to be a "land of opportunity."

The Educational Commission for Foreign Medical Graduates (ECFMG) assesses whether physicians graduating from foreign schools are ready to enter programs of graduate medical education in the United States. After completing ECFMG's exam at the United States embassy headquarters in Rangoon, I waited eight weeks for my results to arrive in the mail from the United States. My family had to establish a good relationship with the postman and during that time gave him what amounted to half his monthly income, a weekly "gift" to ensure he would deliver the letter sent by the ECFMG. This man probably earned about nineteen dollars a month. For such workers struggling to feed their families, bribery was a common practice, especially in dealings with the wealthy class.

As soon as I had the results of my exam I took them to the American embassy, a massive white, Colonial-style complex in downtown Rangoon. I was also required to take the English as a Second Language (ESL) test at the embassy before applying for a position in the United States to work as a doctor. I put on a scarf to disguise myself so that no one could take a picture identifying me, or the government would have known I wanted to leave the country and my family and I could have been penalized.

I was escorted into the office of the US ambassador, Edwin Martin, to request his help in securing a job. Fair-skinned and balding, he impressed me as well dressed in his Western-style suit. I also thought he was exceedingly tall, since most of my countrymen and I were much shorter than his six-foot stature.

Mr. Martin recommended that rather than apply under the third preference category for skilled workers, which had a long waiting list, I apply as a "useful person," listed as the sixth preference. The sixth preference category includes "qualified immigrants who are capable of performing specified skilled or unskilled labor, not of a temporary or seasonal nature, for which a shortage of employable and willing persons exists in the United States."

"That is fine with me," I told him. "I will do whatever is needed, whether working as a nurse, as a technician, or in another health-related job."

"How much salary do you expect to make?" he asked me.

With conviction I replied, "As long as I have a place to stay and food, I'll be satisfied." He seemed impressed with my answer and went out of his way to help me.

My medical diploma, which now hangs in my office, states that it was "given to Aisha Simjee, the daughter of Yoosuf Simjee" on November 16, 1968. Mr. Martin laughed when he read that translation, which must have seemed sexist to him. He was looking at a copy of my original diploma, which I had smuggled out of the country so it would not be taken from me. I gave the original to one of our family's security guards for safekeeping and reclaimed the document after its own odyssey to the United States.

I applied for medical positions in Australia, England, Hong Kong, and the United States. Although the other countries were easier to immigrate to, as they didn't require the exam results, after reading about the progression of women in the West in *Time* magazine, I decided that the United States was where I wanted to go.

I knew schoolmates who had gone to South Baltimore General Hospital (now MedStar Harbor Hospital) in Maryland, and I wrote to them to ask that they put in a good word for me with the hospital administrator. I applied there and received an acceptance letter, which I presented to the United States embassy so that it would more quickly issue me a visa. The position, a rotating internship to begin in July 1970, would pay $7,000 a year.

After receiving my visa and the day before leaving the country, I secretly took a taxi to see the dean of my medical school, Dr. U Ba Than, a general surgeon by profession, to say goodbye. He was highly respected throughout the country. His daughter, Khin May Than, was married to the dictator, General Ne Win, but I trusted Dr. U Ba Than. His second wife was a nurse from Long Beach, so he was broader minded than many of his peers, and he was pleased to hear of my plans. As I prepared to leave his house, he offered to give me a ride back home and I gladly accepted. Dr. U Ba Than drove an Aquarius blue Volkswagen Beetle. At that time, the "Bug" was a very prestigious car in Burma, more highly esteemed than most luxury vehicles. Being driven home in this car by this man, who was very well known in our community, caused quite a stir on my street.

I never forgot the advice he offered me as he drove. "Aisha," he said, "no matter where you go, your gender, age, religion, race, and physical appearance will be taken into consideration. You will have to work harder than others to be equal."

I took to heart the wisdom of his words. As a young female from a Muslim family who had brown skin, straight black hair, and brown eyes typical of the Indian race and weighed in at eighty-three pounds, I had to be mentally prepared to work harder than my classmates and colleagues and not become discouraged when I encountered prejudice.

Dr. U Ba Than's insights proved prophetic when applied to my experience and society in general. I was reminded of this advice during the 2008 presidential race in which we had a woman, Hillary Clinton; an elderly man, John McCain; a Latter Day Saint, Mitt Romney; and an African-American man, who would become President Barack Obama.

Although we have come a long way, Dr. U Ba Than's words still ring true. I am forever grateful to him for strengthening my resolve and preparing me for a journey to the other side of the world.

Microbiologist Louis Pasteur, remembered for monumental breakthroughs in the causes and preventions of diseases, was absolutely correct when he stated, "Chance favors only the prepared mind."

2
America

*Obstacles are those frightful
things you see when you
take your eyes off the goal.*
HENRY FORD

When I was twenty-six years of age I left Burma, knowing I was leaving for good. I realized that I might not ever see my family again. I could see the grief and worry in my stoic father's eyes as I prepared to leave. Although my parents kept their fears to themselves, their faces told me they were worried about how I would be treated. My father was especially heavy-hearted about being prohibited from sending me off with any money due to government regulation.

"May Allah protect you," my teary-eyed mother managed to say as we hugged goodbye. I took a deep breath and boarded a small plane to leave the country with only one suitcase and no money other than a ten-dollar voucher issued by the US embassy. I clutched my visa, my contract with the hospital, and a film of my chest x-ray. The embassy required that I have a physical exam, and because I had been exposed to tuberculosis during my training and tested positive, the film was necessary proof that I was not contagious and that the TB was inactive.

The hospital paid for my flight. At that time, 1970, there were only two destinations out of Burma: Bangkok or Bangladesh (then East

Pakistan). I flew from the latter to London aboard a massive, double-decker Pan American 747 airliner on its maiden flight across the Atlantic.[1] I marveled at its spacious interior, with a lounge that looked like a family room. The thrill of being a passenger on this new, American-made jet helped distract me from the nervousness I felt about starting over in a strange new land. I chose to think of my auspicious flight as a good omen, representing just what was possible as I embarked on my future.

On May 28, 1970, I arrived at Flushing Airport in New York. Upon showing my medical history, required of immigrants at the port of arrival, officials at the airport concerned about my positive TB test placed me in quarantine for several hours. This caused me to miss my connecting flight to Baltimore and lose my luggage.

Finally, I was cleared and on my way to LaGuardia Airport—by helicopter. From there I took a small plane to Baltimore and arrived well into the evening. Because I was so late arriving, no one from the hospital was there to pick me up as planned. I found a taxi driver and showed him my ten-dollar embassy voucher. He escorted me to the taxi office since he had never seen such a voucher. I ended up exchanging the voucher with the manager of the taxi office, and after some discussion among the drivers, one came forward to take me to the hospital. When we arrived, the driver gave me back two dollars. He probably realized I didn't have any money.

Running on adrenaline after an exhausting trip, I entered the hospital only to find that the hospital administrative staff had long since gone home for the night. I explained my story to the hospital operator, which was not an easy task given my thick accent. Finally, I was taken to an on-call room where I could sleep.

The next morning I found my way to the operating room and asked a nurse for scrubs, since my suitcase had not yet been recovered by the airline. Ten days later it finally arrived, much to my relief. A sticker on the bag showed it was from Burma, and the airlines had mistakenly sent it to Bermuda.

I explained to the hospital administrator that I didn't have any money; I asked if I could eat in the hospital cafeteria and have the cost deducted from my salary. He agreed. I was given the key to an on-call room with a couple of beds. I stayed there for the next year, sharing my accommodations with other women doctors, primarily obstetricians who came in at all hours to deliver babies.

My thick accent made me difficult to understand, which frequently caused me to feel insecure and embarrassed. The chief of the medical staff, Robert Parker, MD, was very compassionate. He arranged for me to take accent-reduction classes, along with some of the other interns. The classes eased my discomfort, particularly in sounding out words with *d*, *th*, *v*, and *w*, which I found difficult to pronounce since there are no exact equivalents in the other languages I speak.

Missing my family in Burma and wanting to reassure them that I was safe and well, I wrote letters as often as time permitted. I had to be very careful what I told them as all mail coming to Burma from the United States was monitored. I never mentioned anything negative about Burma or how much better conditions were in the United States.

I also kept in touch with several doctors from Burma, former schoolmates of mine who were working throughout the United States. We shared our experiences through letters, phone calls, and with those working locally, in social gatherings. It was comforting for us to talk about the variety of foods so different from the boiled rice and shrimp or fish sauce we'd always eaten or the challenge of using a fork, when in our homeland we always ate with our hands. We shared with each other about working and helping patients. A common problem for us was speaking English clearly. If a patient didn't understand us, we were advised by our more established counterparts to write out the diagnosis or instructions. At least the patients and families would know we were trying our best to communicate with them.

I appreciated how completely different hospital conditions were in the United States as compared with Burma. Cleanliness was vastly improved, and doctors here were expected to be nice to patients—a very different approach in bedside manner. In Burma's government-run hospitals, physicians had little bedside manner training or time to explain conditions or prognoses to the patients.

During my internship in Baltimore, I applied for a residency in ophthalmology. My medical advisors recommended that I have second and third choices. I was told ophthalmology was one of the most difficult specialties in which to find a residency, and even more so for foreign graduates. Fourth-year local medical students had priority.

Furthermore, many people at that time, as well as today, had never heard of or knew very little about the remote country of Burma, in spite of the fact that it is home to 50 million people. Few if any Burmese people had applied to their institutions. But in spite of these obstacles, I had made up my mind: I was going to specialize in ophthalmology.

While I waited for a residency, I found an ophthalmology research position working for Maurice Edward Langham, PhD, associate professor of ophthalmology and director of research at the Wilmer Eye Institute at Johns Hopkins Hospital and School of Medicine in Baltimore, Maryland. This ophthalmology program was rated number one in the country.

Each week I would go to the basement of the Woods Research Building on the Johns Hopkins campus to anesthetize and measure the pressure in the eyes of cats and rabbits after applying different drugs (no animals were sacrificed). Never having been exposed to how research is conducted in the United States and how papers are written, this work was a valuable part of my education.

Although Dr. Langham was highly regarded in his field, it depressed me to work for him because of his derogatory remarks. It stung when he repeatedly stated that based on his experience in his native London, Indian doctors are good book learners, but not smart enough to be good research physicians. It made no difference to him that I worked diligently or that I was from Burma. He could not get past his prejudice over my Indian ancestry.

"He should never make such remarks," I'd fume. "He should know that strengths and weaknesses exist in every ethnicity represented in medicine." Then and now, legions of Indian doctors excel at all levels and in all specialties, from medical academics and research to the operating table and bedside.

In 1971 there were 130 ophthalmology programs in the country, and I applied to nearly all of them. The only ones I did not consider were those run by the United States Army or Navy or as public health programs because I was not yet a citizen and not eligible for a residency with those programs.

I received four responses asking for more information, and three of the programs granted me interviews. On one interview in Pittsburgh, a well-meaning gentleman, the ophthalmology department chair, invited me to sit down and proceeded to tell me, "I think you'd make a good pediatrician. I'm setting up an interview for you with that department while you're in town." I never went to that interview. Instead, I took the first available Greyhound bus back to Baltimore.

3
Washington, DC,
to California

The farther backward you can look,
the farther forward you can see.
WINSTON CHURCHILL

Because of my work at Johns Hopkins and an intern who at the last minute decided to study orthopedics rather than ophthalmology, in 1972 I was offered an interview and subsequently a position in Washington, DC, at Freedmen's Hospital. Transferred to Howard University Hospital in 1967 after more than one hundred years of operation, Freedmen's Hospital began by caring for freed, disabled, and aged blacks in the District of Columbia and continued its work throughout the next century. During my time there, we served a large volume of patients coming for ophthalmology care.

I moved to a one-bedroom apartment in Hyattsville, Maryland, a place about six miles from the hospital in Washington, DC, and bought a small, red Toyota Corolla. It was the least expensive car available at $2,283 and one of the first foreign cars sold in America. I went to driving school to learn how to operate my automobile since, like most girls where I grew up, I had never learned to drive.

As part of my three-year residency I did a rotation through DC General Hospital under the supervision of Georgetown University

Hospital, a very large and busy medical center with students from three medical schools—Georgetown, Howard, and George Washington University. This incredibly busy institution felt comfortable to me as it reminded me of Rangoon General Hospital.

My residency training also included a three-month rotation through the Department of Ophthalmic Pathology at the Armed Forces Institute of Pathology, one of the world's largest ophthalmic pathology research facilities. I had the privilege of working under the supervision of its chairman of ophthalmic pathology and an internationally renowned giant in the field, Lorenz Zimmerman, MD. An ocular pathologist, Dr. Zimmerman was doing pioneering research on retinoblastoma, a cancer of the retina that afflicts children. I asked him lots of questions and learned a great deal from him. I frequently stayed around at the end of the day to speak with him, not wanting the other residents to think I was asking stupid questions. He could see that I intensely wanted to learn and I took my work very seriously.

One day, Dr. Zimmerman sat me down and explained how ten years earlier, when he was already doing research in retinoblastoma, his own child was diagnosed with this rare cancer. He told me kindly, "Aisha, we have to take life the way it comes." I realized it was his way of telling me to "lighten up," and I began to relax a little, at least in front of him.

Retinoblastoma is easily diagnosed. The most visible symptom is a white pupil. After three and a half decades in practice, I have seen retinoblastoma in only two patients. One was a little girl in Afghanistan. Her mother told me she had seen the white pupil develop in her other three children, who had all died. I took the girl to a physician in Kabul. Her condition was too advanced and her prognosis too poor for me to help her during my short stay there. I took pictures of her and sent them to Wills Eye Institute in Philadelphia, Pennsylvania, where a retina cancer specialist, Jerry Shields, MD, planned to publish them with my permission in his book on retinoblastoma.

With my residency nearing completion, I applied and was accepted for fellowship training in corneal and external diseases at Wills Eye Hospital. That was followed by a second fellowship in eye pathology at Scheie Eye Institute at the University of Pennsylvania. I felt that with these two subspecialty fellowships from such highly respected programs, I would have no problem being hired by a university program. I didn't plan to go into private practice. In Burma, only the very best students were employed by medical schools and teaching hospitals, and I aspired to be the best. I have to admit that at the same time, thinking about the rigors of running my own practice was intimidating. Little did I know at the time that through private practice I would find great satisfaction and enjoyment in treating a variety of patients and developing personal relationships with them.

My academic appointment as an assistant professor of ophthalmology at Howard University in Washington, DC, began in July 1977. By then I had passed my exam with the American Academy of Ophthalmology and earned board certification. But after eight years in the Northeast, I'd had enough of cold weather. My new goal was to move to Southern California, where the climate is comparable to that of Burma.

I moved to Orange, California, in January 1978 and joined the practice of (the late) Joseph Tirico, MD. Always dressed in a suit and tie, he was an ophthalmologist as well as an ear, nose, and throat specialist. I also worked at the University of California Irvine (UCI) Medical Center one and a half days each week as a volunteer attending physician, hoping I would be hired. I continued volunteering there for the next thirty years, although I reduced my time to once a month until 2009, when I felt that UCI no longer needed my services.

Working for Dr. Tirico I earned $1,500 a month. I couldn't afford a vehicle. Before leaving the East Coast, I had given my aging car to a family in need, so I moved to an apartment that was within walking distance of the office, which was on the campus of St. Joseph Hospital in Orange. I was the second female ophthalmologist on its medical staff.

I was the thirteenth associate to join Dr. Tirico's practice of about forty years. The high number of associates was probably due to the fact that he expected us to take calls around the clock, and he was very conservative in his practice, not willing to adopt new procedures. I eventually became the first doctor in his office to perform an intraocular implant, which is today very common practice.

From the time I interviewed for medical staff membership, I noticed curious glances and sly, secretive smiles and smirks from clinicians around the hospital. After nearly four months, I asked Dr. Tirico's secretary, Doreen Hines, and optician, Jean Budd, about it. They told me that the twelfth of Dr. Tirico's associates had turned out to be transsexual, which was nearly unheard of at that time.

Richard Raskind, MD, was a pediatric ophthalmologist who trained at the University of Rochester in New York. He married a model and fathered a son before divorcing, having sex reassignment surgery, and moving to California to begin a new life as Renee Richards, MD. Dr. Richards was an excellent tennis player and competed in tennis tournaments, including one in La Jolla, California, which prompted a San Diego reporter to look into her past and file a story about the winner of the women's tournament being a man. The salacious story went national, garnering Dr. Richards a great deal of attention.[1]

Dr. Tirico was quite agitated about the deception and exasperated with himself for not having realized this very tall person was transgender. Many of his older patients were also upset. Dr. Richards was so embarrassed that she left the practice. She later became a coach for tennis great Martina Navratilova and went on to be inducted into the USTA Eastern Tennis Hall of Fame.

Although petite at four feet eleven inches, as well as married, I sensed that some people were amused and curious to see another female physician join Dr. Tirico's practice. Thank goodness I became pregnant within the year, putting an end to people's speculation about me!

In the months prior to my move to the West Coast, my parents in Burma were pressing me about finding a man to marry. I told them, "I have no time to look for a husband!" My response didn't deter them. They asked my brother, Latif, who had immigrated to Canada, to look for a husband for me.

Two months after I moved to California, Latif called and invited me to visit and meet his friend, a lab technician at a hospital in Toronto. "Sabi Dadabhai is a good man from a good family in India," he assured me. I agreed to come and meet the man who had been orphaned; raised by his grandmother in the small village of Kathor, India; and immigrated to Canada.

I flew there and spent two hours in Latif's house getting to know Sabi. While I found him to be an attractive gentleman, I insisted upon one condition if we were to be married. "You must go to school," I told him, knowing his bachelor's degree from India carried little weight in the United States. Sabi promised he would go back to school and complete his bachelor's degree, and he was true to his word. That promise was critical in my decision to marry him because, I reasoned, if both of us were degreed we could make it. He became a full-time student at UCI, and eventually went to the University of California, Los Angeles (UCLA), where he completed dual master's degrees in business administration and public health (MBA/MPH). He stayed near the UCLA campus five days a week, finished his degree in three years, studied to take the certified public accountant exam, and passed it.

Although I spent just two hours with him and spoke with him only a couple of times on the phone before we married, I felt we would be a good match, and we have been. While arranged marriages may seem to be a strange custom to Westerners, those who are committed to building a life together find they grow to love and respect one another, as happened for Sabi and me.

While my husband went to school, I settled into my profession. Dr. Tirico was seventy-two years old when I joined his practice. A year and a half later he told me he was retiring and would sell me his practice for $65,000. I had barely enough money to support my family, and that was a large amount for me, but Dr. Tirico wanted nothing up front. I agreed, and with a handshake we sealed our deal. I had just enough money to pay him each month and take care of my growing family.

Frequently in the early morning or evening in the office building where I worked, I rode the elevator with an orthopedic surgeon named Milton Legome, MD. I went to him to ask for a loan to buy the practice. "Without collateral the banks won't give me the time of day," I admitted. "But you know I'm dependable and hardworking, and I will pay you back." Fortunately, Dr. Legome agreed to loan me the money. It took me twenty years to pay him back, and I was never late with my monthly payments.

Three days after his retirement, Dr. Tirico called to tell me he was sorry he had sold me his practice. He said that he was "going nuts" at home, with his beloved wife driving him crazy. I told him not to be sorry but to come back to work! Some of his patients were leaving the practice because a pregnant foreign woman operating on their eyes was difficult for them to accept. I told him if he would join me for cases in the operating room, I would give him half of what I earned.

Six months into our arrangement, Dr. Tirico told me he planned to visit his brother in New Jersey. As of late he had been looking pale, and I was concerned. "Before leaving, you must have a checkup," I insisted. He did, and he was diagnosed with lymphoblastic leukemia, a type of cancer that normally manifests in children.

Dr. Tirico ended up in the hospital's intensive care unit. When he had a breakout of herpes zoster, also known as shingles, we knew his immune system had been destroyed and he wasn't going to survive. He never made it to New Jersey.

◆ ◆ ◆

When I joined Dr. Tirico's practice I was thirty-four years old. I didn't want to wait any longer to have children, and within months of my marriage I conceived. Dr. Tirico had worried that because I was pregnant I would take a lot of time off, but I worked until the day before I delivered. (John Christensen, the gentleman I operated on that day, and his wife, Andy, remain my patients to this day, more than three decades later.) Our first daughter, Alia, was followed by her sister, Sufia, just eleven months later.

In 1979, a week after my firstborn arrived, my parents came to the United States to live with me. In the summer of 1975 I had become a US citizen and was able to buy their tickets to bring them to California from Bangladesh, where they had moved a few years earlier to be near my sister and her family, escape a multitude of political problems in Burma, and live in peace.

With my mother able to help care for my baby, I returned to work just two weeks after the delivery. My mother did the cooking and my father helped with my bookkeeping, and together they watched television to learn English. They continued to live with me for several years until they passed away in their seventies.

Within three years, I sent legal papers to the American embassy in Burma and Bangladesh so that my brother, Latif, his wife, and their six children, who lived in Canada, could come to the United States. When they arrived, we had people sleeping everywhere in our three-bedroom house. My brother was able to find a job, and a year or so later he and his wife rented their own place and all eight of them moved to Garden Grove, California.

Soon after my brother was established, I also sponsored my sister Rabia, her husband, and their seven children. They lived with us for a few months, and her oldest daughter, Salma, stayed for a year. She was very bright and went on to become a dermatologist, scoring in the ninety-seventh percentile on her board exam. She has practiced in the

Fresno, California, area for more than twenty years. Another of Rabia's daughters, Saeeda, became an internal medicine physician. Salma and Saeeda earned enough money to put their two younger brothers through dental school at Harvard University. One is an orthodontist and the other a periodontist, both living in Orange County. Rabia's youngest daughter, Nasima, went to work as an equity analyst for Fiduciary Trust Company on the ninety-sixth floor of the World Trade Center, South Tower. On 9/11 she lost her life, along with nearly 600 coworkers.

Another of my sisters, Halima, and her husband came from Burma with their five children in 1982, and stayed with me for about six months. Two of their sons work as handymen, another runs a print shop in Fullerton, California, and one is a school bus driver for disabled children. Their daughter works as a statistician. Although they had been the first of my family to apply for a permit to leave Burma, they were the last to make it here. Because they had a house and money, the government made it difficult for them to leave. They finally had to give up everything and move to a poor area close to Rangoon in order to immigrate.

The last child I sponsored came in 1989. I received a letter from the wife of my cousin, asking me to adopt their seventeen-year-old daughter, Tin Tin Lwin. Going against the cultural norm, my cousin had married a Chinese woman. I was happy to have their sweet and pretty Indo-Chinese daughter stay with us. I found her a job working as a home healthcare assistant for a disabled Caucasian woman in nearby Anaheim. Tin Tin Lwin would cook and clean and watch television with this woman, which helped her learn English more quickly. However, Tin Tin Lwin and her charge watched soap operas, which gave her a rather distorted view of Americans. "They're crazy people," she half-jokingly told me one day not long after she had begun to comprehend what the actors were saying. She subsequently graduated from Cypress College and became a certified home healthcare nursing assistant. Through the Burmese-American community in Southern California, she met a man from Burma, married him, and moved to Culver City, California.

My second cousin Sabiha Vahed was a vibrant seventeen-year-old when she came to America with her parents in 1980. I often used to baby-sit Sabiha while living in Burma. My young charge had always been a beauty, with her wide smile and warm, long-lashed brown eyes. She grew to be much taller than me, and over the years and miles we remained as close as sisters. In 1980, two years after moving to Chicago, Illinois, Sabiha developed severe breathing difficulties. When I called her, she was unable to speak and responded to questions by tapping into the phone. Although biopsies were sent to twenty respected doctors worldwide, no one was able to accurately diagnose her problem.

After she had been in the hospital for four and a half months, I received a call from Sabiha's sister. Sabiha had taken a turn for the worse. Her lungs had collapsed, but her family didn't have the heart to sign Do Not Resuscitate (DNR) documents. They asked me to come to say goodbye and sign the DNR. And so, six days after the birth of my second daughter, I left my baby in the care of my husband and parents and flew to Sabiha's bedside. While I was with her, she took her final breath. We buried her on Christmas Day.

As heart wrenching as this was, I maintained my composure in front of her parents. To bring her family comfort, I promised that I would work to honor her memory. I vowed that in her name I would take care of other young people, and that is what I have done, for her, for Nasima, and for others in my life who have met with a tragic end.

Another cousin, Sakina Simjee, and her husband Elyas Abowath immigrated to Diamond Bar, California. In 1985 Richard Ramirez, a serial killer known as the Night Stalker, murdered Elyas in his bed. He left Sakina a widow with two children, ages three years and three months.

Along with my family members, the loss of some dear friends has motivated me to seize my time for a life of purpose. One of them was

Michael Sein, MD, who was in premedical and medical school in Burma at the same time as I was. Dr. Sein became a radiologist and eventually moved to Orange County to practice. Tragically, in 2008 he lost his life when a drunk driver rammed his Aston Martin as he and his wife sat at a red light in Newport Beach.

Like families everywhere, we have not been immune to tragedy, yet except for Sabiha, Nasima, and Elyas, all my relatives have thrived and are very grateful to be in the United States. As I sponsored my nieces and nephews, they became like my own children. I'm glad I could model for them a good work ethic, and each has become a productive, contributing member of society. When asked how many children I have, I will always proudly reply, "Twenty-one."

4
Guyana

Don't go where the path may lead,
go instead where there is no path
and leave a trail behind.
RALPH WALDO EMERSON

By 1988 I was well established in my practice and my family was thriving. But conditions in my homeland seemed to be deteriorating even further. With apprehension and feelings of helplessness, my family and I read and watched on television disturbing reports about hundreds of thousands of monks, students, and young workers demonstrating against Burma's government. I felt like I'd been punched in the stomach when I learned that outside the Rangoon Institute of Technology, just a few miles from my former home, at least three thousand citizens were massacred by the military junta during a protest.

Spurred by my grief over the suffering in my native land, a great appreciation for the freedom I enjoyed in America, my promise to Sabiha's family, and what I can only describe as a call from a higher power, I began to think about how I could use my skills to help hurting people who have so little in other parts of the world. In 1991, when my daughters were nine and ten years of age, my instincts told me they were old enough for me to leave them in my family's care so that I could pursue medical missions.

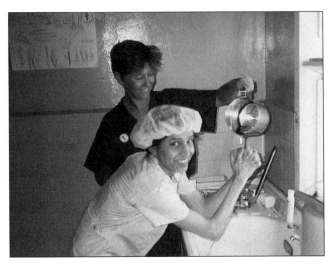

A vascular nurse from Australia pours water obtained from a bucket. The sink had no running water. *Photo courtesy of Aisha Simjee*

That year I contacted Harry Brown, MD, a Santa Barbara, California, ophthalmologist and the founder of Surgical Eye Expeditions (SEE) International,[1] and Baillie Brown, then SEE's executive director, to offer my services. Dr. Brown, at that time in his early sixties, has an impressive background in international eye care. I learned from him that after his premed studies in Missouri, Dr. Brown served as an officer on a battleship in the US Navy at the end of the Korean War. While an intern at Naval Hospital Camp Pendleton in Southern California, he decided to use medicine as a broad base from which he could do other things. He accepted a position with the Central Intelligence Agency as a medical officer in Washington, DC; subsequently opened a general practice in Riverside, California; then went on to do eye training at Jules Stein Eye Institute at UCLA, where he became interested in international ophthalmology.

"That resulted in my taking a trip around the world for a year with my four children, wife, and mother, starting with six months in South Africa," he fondly recalled. "What we saw was right out of *National Geographic*, with witch doctors in leopard skins and eagle feathers throwing the bones. Working with a team from the South African National Council for the Blind, we would go to rural areas and stop at general stores and missionary churches, where we would examine anywhere from ten to three hundred patients, specifically looking for those who were blind in both eyes. It was a museum of pathology. We'd line them up and go down the row with a flashlight, looking for the white pupils. Candidates for cataract surgery would be loaded into our van, and we'd take them back to our clinic for a thorough exam. If they were otherwise healthy we would operate on one eye and in thirty minutes make profound life changes so that they could be productive members of society and their caretakers would be free to go back to work as well."

Dr. Brown's work led him to found SEE International in 1974. After nearly four decades, the organization has been responsible for an estimated four hundred thousand sight-preserving and sight-restoring surgeries. In 2011 alone, SEE organized 140 medical missions, with board-certified, volunteer ophthalmologists performing about fifteen thousand surgeries.

For my first trip, Dr. Brown asked me to travel to Lethem, Guyana (formerly known as British Guiana), located on the northern coast of South America. SEE had been invited there by an organization called Raleigh International for their Operation Raleigh project, which was building a school, latrines, and other facilities to benefit the local people. (Both sending and receiving organizations are needed to organize and host medical mission trips.)

I purchased my own airline ticket, as occurs with almost all mission trips. That expense was minimal compared with the loss of business during a week or more away from my medical practice, where expenses continued. But I felt compelled to go, to give back by doing what I could to restore sight and self-sufficiency.

I deployed with Douglas Katsev, MD, a UCLA-trained ophthalmologist practicing in Santa Barbara, and his wife, Nina Katsev. The three of us went by way of Trinidad. Officials there held our luggage, which contained our personal belongings as well as medical supplies. We stayed at the airport for eight hours until we paid a bribe of $550 for the return of our goods. However, Pan American lost both Nina's luggage and Doug's, and in spite of our efforts to track it down, it was never recovered. I sympathized with them, knowing from experience how disconcerting it was to arrive in a foreign land without one's belongings. Fortunately, in their carry-on bags each had packed a pair of scrubs, which they wore for the duration of the trip.

For whatever reason, the flight we'd booked never arrived to take us, and new arrangements had to be made. We finally managed to make it to Georgetown, the capital of Guyana. Promptly after arriving, we boarded a canary-yellow, six-passenger charter plane for an hour-plus flight into the jungle town of Lethem.

Located beside the Takutu River, Lethem forms a border with Brazil, and just beyond that are the Amazon River and equator. Flying low in the air, we surveyed the vast maze of jungle, winding rivers, and, near Lethem, a golden savannah stretching for miles with few man-made disturbances.

We landed at Lethem's one-runway airport. A friendly young Englishman volunteering with Raleigh International picked us up in a goldenrod sport-utility vehicle and drove us on a rugged, one-lane road to our destination.

The area we would be visiting had no ophthalmologist, so one came from Georgetown to help us and stay for postoperative care. Our group lodged in a former ranch house—the new school that was not yet in use. I wondered if it would ever fully serve its purpose given the practices and priorities of the local culture. By the time the children of the area's tribes reached adolescence, the boys were needed to hunt and fish to provide food for their families, while the daughters' job was to carry water from the river and do household chores.

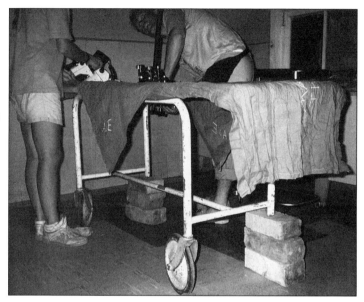

Mounting a microscope on a makeshift operating room table. *Photo by Aisha Simjee*

Soon after arriving, one of the young female volunteers came running out of the school's restroom screaming, "Snake!" I was curious about the serpent causing the commotion and went to see it for myself. The olive-green snake was at least ten feet long, stretched out on the counter behind the sink. I couldn't tell what kind of snake it was, but I knew it was not a cobra or viper. I had seen many of those in Burma, a land full of snakes. Perhaps it was a green anaconda, a species common to the area. We relieved ourselves outside until the next day, when the creature had decided to move on.

While Nina and I wore blue scrubs and our team members sported shorts and T-shirts, most of the local women wore colorful, modest cotton dresses. The men and children who came from the more remote areas surrounding Lethem wore very little clothing in this hot, humid climate.

Lethem was in those days very remote—the most remote place I have visited to this day. After dark the rainforest would come alive with screeching, squawking, quacking, and rustling noises. At times I wanted to pinch myself to be reminded I was still on the same planet.

The rudimentary settlement sat on the bank of the brown, muddy river. Amerindian patients came to see us by way of wooden boats. They lived on their boats for six months out of the year because their houses would be flooded during the rainy season. The time they arrived at our makeshift clinic and the time it was safe for them to leave depended upon the flow of the river. While staying with us, they slept outdoors in hammocks hung from trees and latched wherever possible to the outside walls of the school.

A nurse who came with us told the locals that I was forty-five years old. A dozen or so elementary-age schoolchildren came to behold this "ancient wonder" for themselves. Most had never encountered a forty-five-year-old woman, let alone one who was working! Yellow fever, cholera, and malaria claimed their lives at an early age.

Our Raleigh coworkers were an international group of young people, ages seventeen to twenty-seven. Older people were not allowed to volunteer for this organization, primarily because the difficult living conditions they found on mission trips were best tolerated by youths in the prime of health.

One of the volunteer team members I worked with was an exceptionally beautiful and poised young woman, slender and tall with long dark hair. She worked very hard during our stay. I finally asked her, "What kind of work do you do back home?"

"I was a Christian Dior model in an exclusive shopping area in London called Piccadilly Circus, but I gave it up to volunteer for the past four and a half months, knowing this was my last chance to do so," she said matter-of-factly. "I'm turning twenty-eight soon and will be considered too old to volunteer."

The indigenous people spoke only their native language. Two interpreters helped us as we gave injections of anesthesia to perform

Recovering from surgery, patients—most without a pair of shoes—made their beds and cooked their meals just outside of the clinic. *Photo by Aisha Simjee*

the necessary surgical interventions. To brace themselves before their procedures, the patients would clasp their hands together on their chest, with their elbows lifted to chest height and their teeth clenched.

We performed about thirty cataract surgeries that week for the vision impaired and provided medications for patients with various eye infections. The ranch-house-turned-school wasn't outfitted for medical procedures, so we placed our surgical supplies in plastic bags and taped them to the wall to keep them sterile. Tables missing legs were propped up with bricks. One team member's main job was to stand by a backup generator. Although the building did have electricity, it turned on and off sporadically.

Restoring sight and protecting vision for the Guyanese was a thrilling affirmation for me of the transformational power of medical missions. Yet for all our good work, I also had to accept that there were definite limits to our capabilities. During my stay, I examined a young pregnant girl who could not have been more than fifteen years of age. This age of motherhood was not uncommon there since the people did not have the means to prevent pregnancy. She seemed near full term and had such a large belly that I strongly suspected she was carrying twins. I found that she had toxemia of pregnancy, a grave condition for both mother and child, and her baby's breech presentation was also troubling. After listening to her heart, I also diagnosed pericarditis, an inflammation of the sac surrounding the heart. I remembered it from my days in medical school and in my internship.

Because of her life-threatening condition, preeclamptic toxemia, I felt I should do a Cesarean section to save the baby or babies. A trip to the hospital in Georgetown from Lethem took six and a half hours, and I didn't think she would survive the trip. However, my team leader didn't feel comfortable with me doing a C-section. "If there are any complications, we won't be able to prove we had made the right decision," he reasoned. Instead, the girl was put on a bus that would take her to the hospital. I was shaken to hear that she died on the bus a few hours later.

Patients receiving surgical intervention for eye conditions didn't spend much time convalescing. I would see them wearing their eye bandages as they hauled brush to burn and cooked meals over outdoor fires.

The night before our departure, we gathered with the volunteer staff and patients for a final meal together. Because of the good work of Operation Raleigh, even the prime minister of Guyana came to the farewell dinner to express his appreciation. The natives brought us a plate of what the interpreter said was tiger meat. Strips salted and suspended from a rope to dry, their delicacy was not unlike the beef jerky that originated in South America. This was either puma, which the locals refer to as deer tiger, or jaguar, also referred to as tiger.

"Tiger meat is only given to honorable guests by the chief of the tribe," the interpreter assured me as I eyed the plate. So as not to offend them, I took and ate a tiny piece. "Thank you," I said, with a slight bow to the weathered chief. His plain clothes revealed a European influence, yet his features bespoke his aboriginal, African, and Indian ancestry. He watched expectantly as I dutifully chewed. "Please tell him it tastes good, even though I'm primarily a vegetarian," I instructed the interpreter, which prompted a wide smile and nod from the otherwise solemn chief.

After nearly a week in Lethem, we headed back to the airport, where ferocious-looking dogs would bare their teeth if a stranger dared approach our boxed microscopes, sterilizers, and other instruments. A sign posted nearby read, "Warning: Guard Dog on Duty—Survivors will be prosecuted."

Unfortunately, our flight out on Pan American Airlines never happened because while we were in Guyana, the airline declared bankruptcy and shut down. Instead, we flew by small plane to the island of Trinidad. The trip leader was a Rotary Club member, and consequently we stayed overnight at the home of another club member. With the help of the American embassy in Georgetown, we purchased very expensive one-way tickets and returned home the following day.

I reported back to Dr. Brown, "I'd say the trip was a success, and I'm glad I went."

"I heard about the snake by the sink and how you took it in stride," he commented. "I know it was rough out there, but you didn't complain about anything. By golly, lady, you've got spunk!"

In spite of our travel difficulties and a challenging environment, I knew I had done some good. It seems I had fallen in love with helping those who cannot help themselves. Mission trips were now a part of my calling, and this would be the first of many mission trips. A year later, I left for El Salvador.

5
El Salvador

Live so that when your children think
of fairness and integrity,
they think of you.

H. JACKSON BROWN, JR.

In 1992, humanitarian Dr. Harry Brown, SEE executive Baillie Brown, an ophthalmologist from Costa Rica, his nurse, and I responded to a request to SEE International for vision aid from an organization in El Salvador called FUDEM Direct Relief.

I rendezvoused with the Browns in El Salvador's capital and largest city, San Salvador. From there we took a car for a nearly five-hour drive northwest to Santa Ana, the country's second largest city. Every time the car had to stop, we were surrounded by dozens of beseeching children selling Chiclets and sugar cane.

I stayed for a week in the home of a Guatemalan husband and wife. Thankfully, their simple wooden home had indoor plumbing and was within walking distance of the local hospital. As was the local tradition, I slept on a bamboo mat on the floor. In the few hours I was there each night, I slept soundly.

Annie Maxwell, a wealthy local woman working with FUDEM, organized our visit. On our last day in El Salvador, she welcomed us to her beautiful beach house. There seemed to be about thirty employees on her household staff. I couldn't help but think, *What a striking contrast this is to the widespread poverty I've seen.* Many locals lived in houses made of scraps of wood and corrugated metal. More than half the people in rural areas had virtually no access to clean water or sanitation facilities and struggled just to feed their families.

In a poorly lit and furnished hospital with peeling paint on its walls, I treated a number of young men with traumatic cataracts—a clouding of the lens due to an injury. Patients who have very low vision are classified as "counting fingers," "hand motion," "light perception," and worst of all, "no light perception." A patient with traumatic cataracts typically has only hand-motion vision or light perception.

Rarely on a mission trip do I find time to get to know patients or expend my energies advocating on their behalf. As much as I would like to follow patients' progress and delight with them over their restored vision, in most places I've been, I know that my hours are best spent performing as many procedures as possible in the time allotted.

But on this mission, one of my patients was a fifteen-year-old boy named José whom I will never forget. Until one came close enough to look in his eyes, he looked like a typical teenage mestizo boy with a head of curly brown hair, standing a few inches taller than me. Upon closer inspection, I found bilateral traumatic white cataracts with limited, hand-motion vision.

I removed the cataract from one eye. The reason that I generally correct only one eye is that I won't be around in the coming weeks for the patients' postoperative care to detect any complications or to measure the outcome. One of my professors in Burma used to say, "The first eye is the best teacher for the second eye," meaning only after the first surgery can we know how a patient's system will react.

The next day when I checked on José, he gave me the biggest heart-melting smile. I felt like Santa Claus!

It seemed odd to me that José's parents were not with him. When I asked the hospital staff why that was, I was given the disturbing news

This patient recovers from surgery. I discovered that many of the patients I treated were prisoners. *Photo by Aisha Simjee*

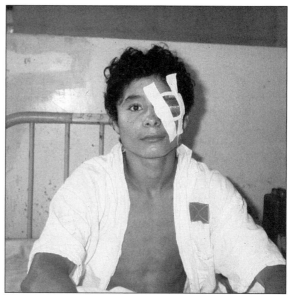

that my patient had been brought to the hospital from the nearby prison.

Salvadoran prisons are notoriously violent, gang-ridden places with horrible living conditions. Due to rampant poverty in El Salvador, care for the masses—let alone its prisoners—was cost prohibitive. The country also lacked medical specialists. Thus, many of the locals' eye problems were left untreated. Also, I suspect that the local ophthalmologists didn't want to treat the prisoners due to a very real possibility of reprisal and revenge from prevalent, ruthless, and highly territorial local gangs.

Still thinking about José, on my last day in Santa Ana I went to see the warden of the maximum-security prison, overcrowded with close to two thousand prisoners that included many of the country's most dangerous criminals and gang members. Keeping my voice soft and controlled in spite of my agitation, I probed politely through an interpreter, "How will José survive in such an environment? Certainly he is not being rehabilitated."

When the warden didn't respond, I continued, "This boy should be in school. He should be sent home to his parents, who can care for him and feed him decent meals." The stone-faced warden patiently heard me out, inclined his head, and replied, "Okay." I can only hope that he took my advice.

6
Thailand

*The road of life contains unplanned
detours, sometimes leading us down
a path which we could not have foreseen.
These new paths are often bumpy,
but family and friends smooth the way.*

JENNIFER SORENSEN

David Paton, MD, started ORBIS International in the 1970s while he was head of the ophthalmology department at Baylor College of Medicine in Texas. His idea was to use aviation to bring aid to a world in which 75 percent of blindness is preventable. His vision was realized when he prevailed upon United Airlines Chairman Edward E. Carlson to donate to ORBIS an out-of-service DC-8 airplane and persuaded philanthropists to fund the project. The plane was converted into a hospital with an operating room and a postoperative recovery area. I found ORBIS to be run as a first-class organization and outfitted with the most updated microscopes and materials.[1]

On the airport property in Bangkok, Thailand, a patient screening and preoperative waiting area and beds would be set up in a large tent where patients could convalesce for two to three days. The plane was fully staffed. Along with paid surgical nurses, it flew with an aeronautic mechanic, electrician, and plumber to bring the hospital's equipment, power, and plumbing online. ORBIS also had its own ophthalmologist on staff, a young doctor recently out of his residency. Another volunteer ophthalmologist from Montana also came on our trip.

Physician volunteers were virtually the only unpaid staff; however, this was the only time my flight was paid for me. If I pay, I find the time to go, but if the sending or receiving organization pays, it says when. With my busy practice at home, this arrangement has rarely worked for me.

We traveled a full day to reach Bangkok. In those days, wherever ORBIS went, the team stayed for three weeks. ORBIS staff and I stayed in a hotel that was the equivalent of a Holiday Inn.

We arrived, in September 1992, to a continuous warm downpour with puddles everywhere we looked. The monsoon rains were so intense and the flooding so heavy that our team couldn't connect the equipment to the local electricity. Instead, the supplies from the plane were moved to five area hospitals where we would perform surgeries. Getting to those hospitals, however, proved very challenging. Bangkok is known for having some of the worst traffic in the world, with its aggressive drivers going too fast, failing to obey traffic signals, and coming within an inch or two of each other on jam-packed streets.

The local hospitals were fairly well equipped, and the local doctors were pleased to see us. At King Chulalongkorn Memorial Hospital, the doctors were excited to see and try our phacoemulsifier machine, which we used for the treatment of cataracts. This ultrasonic device, with its vibrating probe inserted into the eye, breaks cataracts into tiny pieces, like fruit in a blender. Not only has it made cataract surgery minimally invasive, it has helped make cataract surgery one of the world's safest and most effective surgical procedures.

While we did treat a few patients for cataracts and trachoma, most of my time was spent demonstrating and teaching the modern phaco technique to the local ophthalmologists, which was no easy task given our language barrier. One of the doctors was a young woman who had trained at Wills

Eye Hospital in Pennsylvania for a year and knew my mentor from my time there, Peter Laibson, MD. We agreed that we had been fortunate to glean knowledge from him of corneal diseases and cornea transplantation.

While working in the Bangkok hospitals, I ran into two more ophthalmologists whose paths had crossed mine. Pornsawat Nantawan, MD, was trained in retina surgery at Pennsylvania's Scheie Eye Institute while I was there doing my medical retina fellowship. Lalida Pariyakanok, MD, studied after me at Wills Eye Hospital, where I had done my cornea fellowship. Running into Drs. Nantawan and Pariyakanok, I could not help but think, *What a small world!*

Before going to Bangkok, I wrote to an old friend, Watanee Jenchitr, MD. She lived not far from where we were stationed and came by the hospital to say hello. While I was on the East Coast, I became acquainted with Watanee, an ophthalmologist who had trained in New York while her husband trained to be a thoracic surgeon. We had taken our board examinations together. I remember that she and her husband had a baby during that time, and they sent their newborn son back home to her parents to care for so they could complete their educations.

Soon after finishing her training, Watanee returned to Thailand to practice ophthalmology; she went on to train young doctors in the specialty and is today a highly respected Thai ophthalmologist. During our visit, I discovered that she was also passionate about educating young girls so that they could find high-wage jobs and escape prostitution, and she had dedicated her energies to that cause. For her services in championing human rights, she received the King's Medal, the highest honor bestowed in Thailand.

With the rampant, open practice of prostitution, Bangkok has gained notoriety for its human trafficking and sex tourism and, not surprisingly, has reaped one of the world's highest rates of HIV/AIDS. Watanee worked tirelessly to secure educations and jobs for vulnerable young women so that they could be financially independent rather than sexually exploited.

7
Mexico

*You can't live a perfect day
without doing something for someone
who will never be able to repay you.*
JOHN WOODEN

In my office hangs a tan leather clock from a humanitarian trip I took to Chihuahua, Mexico, in 1993. It's fashioned from the head of a drum that was given to me by a local Tarahumara Indian chief for providing eye care to his people, for whom time seems to stand still. Their way of life has changed very little over the past six centuries.

On the fifteenth anniversary of SEE International, I went to Chihuahua along with John Dagianis, MD, of New Haven, Connecticut, and his nurse, Jan. As we became acquainted on the way to our destination, I learned that Dr. Dagianis had trained at Wills Eye Hospital, although not at the same time as I had.

Our mission was to help the people of the Tarahumara Indian Reservation.[1] Locally, there was only one ophthalmologist, Dr. Sergio Morales. He had offered us the use of his operating room and clinic in a two-story stucco building. We lodged just above Dr. Morales's clinic, which eliminated our need for transportation and helped us maximize our time there. The clinic was well organized, having welcomed a few SEE International mission groups in the past.

While some of the more modernized people from nearby villages wore jeans and cowboy-style clothing, most of the women wore long dresses and a few of the men came wearing breechcloths called *zapetas*. Not all of the patients understood or spoke Spanish. Some only spoke the dialect of the Sierra Tarahumara tribe. A native translator worked in the clinic to facilitate our conversations about these patients' medical conditions. The patients were somewhat bashful in their demeanor and didn't ask a lot of questions or offer much information. For those who did speak Spanish, I recall frequently repeating to patients postoperatively, "Yo estoy contenta que sus ojos están cicatrizando bien," meaning, "I am satisfied that your eyes are healing well," and in return receiving big smiles.

The Tarahumara have a low life expectancy,[2] although the reasons for their mortality are quite different than in more modern societies. Certainly the problem isn't fresh air and exercise; these people have a reputation for being among the world's best distance runners. They don't suffer from high rates of cancer, stroke, heart disease, or diabetes as occur in the United States, quite possibly due to our nation's overconsumption of high fat and processed foods. Taras do have a high infant mortality rate, poor resistance to contagious diseases, and minimal access to modern medicine. They start their families early and by the time they are twenty-five years old tend to have several children. Like the people of many cultures, they seemed to think of their offspring as their insurance policy for old age.

Although their ancient culture seemed strange to me, they were very comfortable having me care for them. Like me, they are small in stature, with brown eyes and straight black hair. They had sun-baked faces, high cheekbones, and very small palpebral fissures, or eye openings. This is common for people living high in the mountains and constantly exposed to the hot sun. This exposure leads to early macular degeneration, and I saw a number of patients who had solar maculopathy from the intense sunlight.

"Why," I wondered aloud over a meal of rice and beans with my colleagues, "would they continue living in isolation? Why have they stayed so high in these rugged mountains, where the climate is so harsh, rather than move to the base of the mountain, where it would be easier to farm and find food?"

Dr. Morales shook his head, looking toward the mountains. "Tarahumara in the remote areas have lived for centuries as subsistence farmers, and they're very resistant to change," he said. They're also suspicious that white men and even their fellow countrymen will try to take their land, which is extremely important to them. They suspect these outsiders are always out to get something, to take advantage of them.

After working at the clinic and performing surgeries for a few days, our team planned to fly to a remote part of the reservation located high in the mountains at an approximately seven-thousand-foot elevation. We knew it would be difficult for patients from this region to come to us since it was a seven-hour bus ride each way. I was looking forward to visiting a mountain village and learning more about this ancient, well-preserved culture.

A wealthy man from the city of Chihuahua with a red, single-engine airplane loaded our supplies and set out to take Dr. Dagianis, Jan, and me into the high mountains of Sierra Tarahumara. I had never seen such a plane, let alone flown in one! As we rose into the air, Dr. Dagianis turned to me and with quiet consternation asked, "Did you notice that the pilot has only one working eye?" I had observed that he appeared to have large-angle exotropia, a condition in which the eye deviates outward, resulting in poor vision. I nodded yes and whispered to Dr. Dagianis to keep his voice down.

Because of a thick fog, our plane circled the mountains several times. The pilot couldn't find the landing strip and we were forced to turn back. Once we landed, Dr. Dagianis told me that he spent a good portion of our time in the air saying his prayers.

Instead, a bus brought the people who needed medical attention on the long trip down from the mountain to the clinic, where Dr. Dagianis and I provided surgical care. He retired at midnight, but I kept working until 3:00 a.m., helping as many patients as possible.

This was one of those rare times when I did not see my patients the day after surgery. Dr. Morales reassured me, "Don't worry Dr. Aisha, I'll check on them." The next morning at 7:00 a.m., we said our goodbyes and left by car for the airport.

I've been to so many places, and so far it has been my fate never to be hurt. It's foolish not to be careful, but I don't believe in being afraid, and I wasn't afraid flying over the mountains. After all, is it worthwhile to live a fearful life? Fear is paralyzing, and there is no inoculation for it other than faith.

8
Vietnam

*We could never learn
to be brave and patient,
if there were only joy in the world.*

HELEN KELLER

In 1995, SEE International was invited to Vietnam, and I gladly accepted SEE's request for my assistance on yet another medical mission. I met two other seasoned ophthalmologists, Nibondh Vacharat, MD, of Pennsylvania, and Harry Lebowitz, MD, of Delaware. John Deane, the CEO of a company that made ophthalmology surgical instruments, who wanted to see Vietnam, joined us as our operating room assistant. Our work took us to Ho Chi Minh Eye Hospital.

On our trip to Vietnam we received less than a warm welcome from customs officials. In spite of a letter from the country's Ministry of Health, upon our arrival a customs officer who refused to release our necessary surgical supplies and implants delayed us. Since I was the team leader carrying the supplies from California, I went to the customs office on the following day to assure the officials that our supplies were for charitable purposes and would be used in the hospital. Finally, they charged me one hundred dollars and released our luggage.

The city was divided into districts, and we spent our time working in a hospital in District 3. On this trip I brought instrumentation to perform cornea transplant surgery. At the same time I was there, three Australians from an eye bank in Sydney were traveling through Ho Chi Minh City. The chairman of the hospital informed them that a cornea transplant surgeon was visiting from California. He convincingly told them that I could really use a cornea for the dual purpose of helping restore a patient's sight and showing the local ophthalmologists how a cornea transplant is done. The Australians graciously brought the hospital chairman one cornea well packaged for its preservation.

I began the patient selection process immediately. I proposed that we should perform the procedure on a young patient from the area who could receive follow-up care after the transplant. The hospital lined up twenty-one candidates to select from, and after meticulous screening I chose an otherwise healthy nineteen-year-old girl.

On the day of the surgery, forty or so nurses, doctors, and students crowded into the operating room and its hallway to observe the case. To my knowledge, it was the first cornea transplant performed in that hospital. One female physician had trained in Russia to do cornea transplants, but due to the lack of instruments and needed supplies— including corneas—she hadn't been able to perform any transplantations. She was pleased to observe the case and assured me she would watch the patient closely after I departed. While I was confident that the patient's cornea transplant surgery was successful and we had corrected her extremely poor vision, restoration would be gradual, and her cornea would have to be checked the day following surgery, several times in the next two weeks, at intervals throughout the first year, and annually thereafter. The graft should last a lifetime with prompt attention to any sign of rejection.

When we had finished our cataract surgeries and treatments for pterygium and other eye diseases, my colleagues and I went to see the nearby Cu Chi Tunnels, a complex tunnel the Vietcong once used as their headquarters.

The tunnels of Cu Chi are located at the border of Vietnam and Laos, where the Vietnamese fought the French and later the Americans. One cannot *walk* through the tunnel. Crawling through the small space leads to a conference room where soldiers would hold their meetings. Several holes lead to the surface for fresh air and a firing post. The soldiers would cook meals here as well, but only very small amounts of food at a time so that the rising smoke would not lead to their discovery. The complex even had a well, a storage room, and sleeping space. John Deane tried to make his way through the tunnel but found he was too tall to continue and had to turn back.

After visiting the tunnel, I headed back to the hotel, gathered my belongings, and went back to the airport to return home. Dr. Lebowitz, however, wanted to stay for a few more days and tour Vietnam. Later that year in Atlanta, Georgia, while attending the annual American Academy of Ophthalmology meeting, I ran into Dr. Lebowitz. He told me that after we had said our goodbyes, he had proceeded into Ho Chi Minh City, where he was mugged by a pack of youths. They grabbed his backpack and inside it found his tear gas can and sprayed him in his eyes. They stole the backpack and his money but fortunately left his hotel key, passport, and ticket to fly back home.

The Vietnamese patients and doctors were most appreciative that we had come to lend a hand, and they brought us food and local, handmade crafts as gestures of gratitude. But the customs officials clearly harbored resentment toward Americans, stemming back to the Vietnam War. I sensed that their prevailing attitude was almost as if we owed them this humanitarian work.

Although it's always nice to feel appreciated, that's not what motivates me. The goal of missions is not ego gratification but instead giving a hand to those who desperately need it.

9
Republic of Georgia

If what you have done yesterday
still looks big to you,
you haven't done much today.

MIKHAIL GORBACHEV

In 1997, SEE International contacted me about a request from the United Methodist Committee on Relief to host an ophthalmologist in Kutaisi in the Republic of Georgia. I took out my world map and unrolled it to locate the destination, but Kutaisi was nowhere to be found. I concluded that it must be very remote and small not to be found on my map.

Georgia is bordered by the Black Sea on the west, Turkey and Armenia on the south, and Russia on the north. With less than two hundred thousand citizens, Kutaisi is actually the country's second largest city, located in west-central Georgia and surrounded by forest and mountains.[1] Just eight years earlier, the country had split from the Soviet Union.

I accepted the invitation and found myself on my way to Kutaisi. I was the first physician sent by SEE to Kutaisi, and I was going solo since no one else had volunteered for the trip.

To reach Kutaisi, I flew from Los Angeles to Finland, then on to Tbilisi, Georgia's capital and largest city. At the airport I was met by a gentleman named Kote Kadjaia, a leader of the local Methodist church and the host for my visit. I was pleasantly surprised that he had made all the necessary arrangements for my arrival with the country's customs officials. In spite of my having excessive luggage—large boxes with operating room equipment—not one question was asked. I really appreciated this since I didn't speak a word of the local language.

Unfortunately, my escort spoke almost no English or any other language that I understood. I walked with him to his very small car, but all my supplies were loaded into a van. Kote must have seen trepidation on my face, so he tried to reassure me with hand gestures and the few English words he knew that the luggage would arrive safely and on time.

As he drove through the mountains, more than one hundred miles to Kutaisi, there was no communication between us except for minimal sign language. Followed by the van, we drove for five hours, stopping only once at a small roadside building. When I walked over and opened the door, I discovered it was a restroom run by an elderly peasant woman. I later learned that payment for roadside restroom use is common in Europe.

We finally arrived at Kote's home, set on a picturesque, wooded Kutaisi hillside. He introduced me to his wife, Dr. Gulnara Kadjaia, an anesthesiologist at the local hospital, who welcomed me with open arms. She showed me to the bedroom where I would be sleeping throughout my stay. In it they had placed a beautiful, welcoming bouquet of yellow dahlias.

Fortunately, Dr. Kadjaia spoke some English. Hearing this was a great relief for me, as I realized what a risk I had taken as a woman traveling alone. Looking back, even though I was treated very well, I would not want any female to be so trusting and take such chances as I had taken.

The couple's twelve-year-old daughter, Giga, was studying to be a pianist. During my stay, she and her younger brother, Nino, charmed me by singing for me on several occasions.

Even though I had arrived at their home in the middle of the night, the family was waiting up and insisted that Giga play the piano for me. As her fingers ran up and down the keys, she made beautiful music,

Total corneal opacity, resulting from an infection. *Photo by Aisha Simjee*

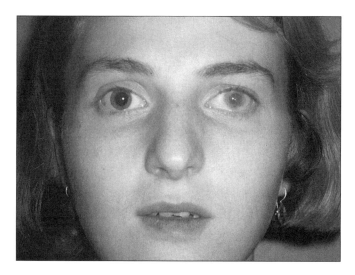

but I hoped she would finish soon as I could barely keep my eyes open. My flight had taken more than nineteen hours and the drive another five. I was exhausted.

The next day, Dr. Kadjaia took me to Kutaisi Church Hospital and gave me a tour of the eye clinic and the operating room. I was dismayed to find the OR looking like a construction zone, with wood planks and dust everywhere. Dr. Kadjaia introduced me to the hospital's chairman of ophthalmology, Dr. Zoumbdulidza, and his lovely daughter, Natasha, who was a medical student in Moscow and an aspiring ophthalmologist. She spoke enough English to pepper me with questions about my career.

During my previsit communication with SEE International, I had been told there would be a microscope at the hospital, which I would need to perform cataract surgeries (although I have performed cataract procedures without one, using a head magnification loop). I looked for it, but the only one in sight was in pieces on the floor.

"Doctor, is this the microscope you promised to have for me to use?" I inquired with concern through the interpreter and social worker, Gegi.

Dr. Zoumbdulidza, who was a very pleasant man, assured me he would quickly put it together and have it in working order.

While he was assembling the microscope, I unpacked my supplies in the poorly lit operating room. I noticed a rice cooker sitting on a counter and asked how it was used. "That's our surgical sterilizer," he relayed. I kept my reservations to myself, not wanting to offend.

When I was nearly finished, a clinic technician knocked on the door and escorted in a seven-year-old girl, along with her mother, so that I could examine her eye. I could see that the girl had a ruptured globe—a tear in the outer surface of the eyeball—and asked through an interpreter what had happened. Through an interpreter the mother explained, "I asked her to milk one of our goats but hadn't warned her not to milk the one who was nursing a kid, and the protective nanny gored her in the eye with its horn!"

The next day when I ventured into the operating room, I was shocked to see that it was in pristine condition, with the equipment in working order. Staff must have worked all night to assemble the equipment and clean the room.

Along with treating other patients, I checked on the girl every day and was happy to find her regaining some sight and improving day by day. Based on my examination, I was confident that there was no chance of sympathetic ophthalmia, an inflammation that can affect both eyes following trauma to one eye. It can leave the patient completely blind within days to several years.

The young mother thanked me profusely and brought me a box of local pastries for treating her daughter, a beautiful child with curly hair and a contagious smile. On my last day there, I took off my blue lapis earrings, which the child had admired, and gave them to her. She seemed happier to receive the earrings than she was that I had fixed her eye!

Throughout my stay all of the people I met were very pleasant, going out of their way to offer assistance and constantly offering me food.

Perhaps they thought I was undernourished because of my size, since all the adults were very tall and big boned. I shared many a meal of goat milk and goat meat. I was exceptionally pleased with the doctors and nurses I worked with in the operating room. They were so polite, constantly smiling and bowing, and always eager to help. Patients and the hospital officials alike brought me flowers of appreciation. The Georgians are known for their genuine hospitality, and it certainly made my work there all the more enjoyable.

During my time in Georgia, I was able to do twenty-six cataract surgeries, all of which were successful in restoring vision. I even operated on a one-hundred-four-year-old woman with light-perception cataracts. I removed the advanced cataract from one eye, and the next day the patient and family were so delighted with her eyesight that they wanted me to perform surgery on her other eye. "I don't want to take that chance," I gently told the family through the interpreter, explaining, "Performing surgery on someone of such advanced age is high risk, and not having a thorough assessment of her overall condition, I don't want to press our luck."

Each day as I arrived at the hospital, I noticed a huge building next door that had no windows and no doors except for the large, gray iron doors at each end of the structure. On my last day in Kutaisi, I asked about the building. I learned that it was used to store the country's arms supplies. In fact, a hospital staff person told me there were enough arms in the building to destroy the entire world in five days. *How ironic*, I thought, *to store weapons next to a place of healing*. But apparently, keeping this arsenal next to a hospital was a protective measure, since most combatants would be less likely to target a hospital.

After I completed my surgical and medical aid and training of local residents, the church administrator offered to show me around the local historic church. It was decorated with ancient mosaics and giant mural paintings and ornamental carvings fit for a museum. I jokingly told him he should sell these treasures to expand their eye clinic.

Because Kutaisi had limited resources for its people's vision care, I left a number of instruments with the hospital staff that I felt they could use. Although I was the first foreign ophthalmologist to travel to Kutaisi to provide vision care, at least one other ophthalmologist from SEE has since followed in my footsteps.

I must say I thoroughly enjoyed my time there. The people were so charming that if I hadn't been needed in other places, I would have gladly gone back. I left very satisfied that I had made a difference in the lives of the Kutaisi people and in a place I had never known even existed before visiting. I left richer for the delightful people I met and the friendships I made.

10
Nigeria

*One of the greatest diseases
is to be nobody to anybody.*
MOTHER TERESA

A small village in Abeokuta, in the southwestern African country of Nigeria, was my next medical mission destination. The name Abeokuta, meaning "refuge among rocks," dates back to the 1800s, when the villagers would scatter and seek shelter from the common enemy—slave traders—in the rocky outcroppings surrounding the city. Abeokuta, a city of around 600,000, is about a two-hour bus ride from the airport in Lagos, a major Nigerian metropolis.

This was the first time my eldest daughter, Alia, accompanied me on a mission trip. She had been asking me for some time to let her come along, but the timing hadn't been right before because of her schooling. In December 1998, she was a student at the University of Pennsylvania, and the trip was during her winter break. Alia was planning to become a doctor, and I agreed it would be a good idea for her to accompany me. She would gain greater appreciation for life outside her privileged world, plus this experience would look good on her applications to medical schools. I myself serve on the UCI School of Medicine Admissions Committee, and I notice such things.

My daughter Alia checking in at the airport with our medical supplies. *Photo by Aisha Simjee*

I tried to mentally prepare Alia for the intense poverty we would find. "Don't expect conditions to be ideal; it's a developing country," I told her on the long flight to Nigeria. Still, she could not help but be saddened by the destitution we encountered. Within those few days, I saw Alia mature what seemed like a year.

As we drove through remote parts of Nigeria, I saw that some of the children had no shoes and were dressed in filthy rags. Back home in Orange County, Alia and her sister frequently added their perfectly good clothing discards to a CHOC Children's Hospital box we kept for donations. After Alia, and subsequently Sufia, accompanied me on medical missions, I noticed that the box filled much more slowly. I also heard far fewer complaints about trivial matters, such as what was for dinner or what was in their wardrobes.

Our trip was arranged by SEE International and hosted by Dr. Kunle Hassan, a prominent vitreoretinal surgeon and the chief medical director

A tribal chief and his wife pause for a picture with Dr. Kunle Hassan, the chief medical director of Eye Foundation Hospital, and me. *Photo courtesy of Aisha Simjee*

of Eye Foundation Hospital in Lagos. We stayed near downtown Lagos, and every day the trip across town to Dr. Hassan's clinic took more than an hour due to horrendous traffic. On a few of those days, an ambulance picked us up. To expedite our commute, we traveled with the siren blaring. It made me cringe with guilt since we didn't have any emergency patients on board.

On one of those days, just outside the clinic I saw a man lying along the roadside and I asked the ambulance driver to stop so we could try to help him. The interpreter and I disembarked and knelt beside the man. I found he could barely see. "He's having difficulty making it to the clinic," the interpreter translated for me. I sent a clinic aide to ask Dr. Hassan's permission for us to pick up the exhausted man and bring him to the clinic. With Dr. Hassan's approval, we linked arms and brought the poor man inside, where I examined him and diagnosed simple white cataracts. I performed cataract surgery to restore his sight—at least enough for him to walk home following his recovery.

On this trip I brought two preserved corneas, which needed to be utilized as soon as possible. Soon after our arrival in Lagos, I found two patients who needed them. One was a twelve-year-old girl. The other patient was a sixty-year-old internist with one good eye who came from a village a seven hour drive from Lagos, where he owned a hospital. He'd heard from Dr. Hassan that I was bringing corneas with me.

Both of the transplant cases were successful, and I treated a few other patients as well. While working in Dr. Hassan's clinic, I also met with local medical students and residents, and four of the physicians in the residency program observed and assisted with the surgeries. During my few hours with them, their eagerness to learn and assist shone in their eyes as we performed cataract and external eye surgeries.

We left our new friends in Lagos the next day, and after a two-hour bus ride to Abeokuta, we disembarked in front of a large Welcome banner. Because there were no hotels in the area, we stayed in the governor's expansive mansion. Outside, young girls awaited our arrival holding flowers, smiling, and waving. As Alia and I were escorted to our massive bedroom, she whispered, "I feel like royalty."

At the local clinic, patient after patient presented with external eye diseases and advanced glaucoma—the result of not having proper eye care, or any care at all, or decent hygiene since clean water was scarce. The children may have been unkempt and the people poor, but they were very sweet and repeatedly thanked us for visiting them.

I must admit to nearly misdiagnosing some of the first preop patients with blue sclera (Nevus of Ota), a rare hereditary defect in which the white of the eye, or sclera, has a bluish appearance. But after seeing the condition repeatedly, I became suspicious and checked the microscope, which turned out to be defective—stuck on a blue light mode—and had to be repaired.

Although the political conditions of the country did not affect our mission, we observed rampant poverty, which usually precedes conflict. It was a luxury in this part of the world to have decent shoes. I was told that Nigeria at that time was considered one of the most corrupt countries in the world. When we returned to John Wayne Airport in Orange County, we saw signs warning travelers that for their safety, they should not fly to Nigeria due to serious "political unrest." A few months after our trip, I read in the newspaper that Nigeria's president, General Sani Abacha, had been found dead. Although never substantiated, it was speculated that he had died from food poisoning.[1]

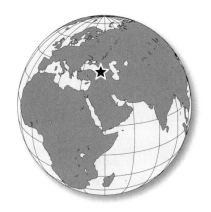

11
Armenia

This is the paradox of vision:
Sharp perception softens
our existence in the world.
SUSAN GRIFFIN

American-born Armenian ophthalmologist Roger Ohanesian, MD, has made semiannual visits to the home of his ancestors since he founded the Armenian EyeCare Project in 1992. As a teenager, he watched as his grandmother became blind after cataract surgery and retina detachment, and the experience motivated him to become an ophthalmologist. In 1999, this distinguished-looking Orange County ophthalmologist with silver hair and thick, dark eyebrows received the Armenia Presidential Award for Service.

That same year, Dr. Ohanesian contacted me to ask if I'd be interested in taking a trip with him and Richard Hill, MD, a local glaucoma specialist. They were arranging the trip with the help of SEE International and the host, Armenian EyeCare Project. I was happy to join them, especially when Tissue Banks International (TBI), a nonprofit organization in Baltimore, Maryland, consented to giving me as many corneas for cornea transplants as were available at the time of my departure. This would be the second time that someone brought corneas to Armenia on a medical mission (Armenian-American doctor Sarkis Soukiasian, MD, of Boston, Massachusetts, brought the first one on a trip to Armenia with Dr. Ohanesian in 1992).

Before we left, I took time to visit St. Mary Armenian Apostolic Church in Costa Mesa, California, to acquaint myself with Armenian culture. The parishioners were friendly and, considering how full the church was that Sunday, the staff was well organized. Attendance at the church was impressive but not too surprising since it was one of only two churches in Orange County for Armenians at that time, and California has the largest population of Armenians outside Armenia. Located east of Turkey and north of Iran, Armenia was a constituent republic of the former Soviet Union known as the Armenian Soviet Socialist Republic. The nation gained its independence in 1991. A severe economic downturn had followed, which not surprisingly led to a lack of proper healthcare.

Just prior to our trip, TBI delivered to my office more than a dozen corneas, bottled in nutrient media and appropriately packaged, gathered from all over the United States. As usual, I hand-carried the well-taped box of precious corneas rather than send them in my luggage, where they could be lost or damaged. In our stopover in Switzerland, it was rather difficult, but I was able to convince the customs officials, who were unfamiliar with cornea transplants, of the value of my cargo and the need for it to be hand-carried.

Armenia officials wanted to run the cornea box through an x-ray machine. No research has been done on whether airport x-ray machines damage the endothelial layer of the cornea, which is the most important part of a successful transplant. While today's increased airport security is warranted, it makes transporting corneas unmolested an even greater challenge. I'm not sure if I'll be able to persuade foreign or domestic customs officials not to subject my cornea boxes to screening in the future.

I actually cried to smooth the way through customs, sensing that a woman's tears could engender the officials' sympathy and cooperation.

I was, in fact, genuinely upset. I pleaded with them, "Please don't risk destroying these corneas. They are the gift of sight for some of your countrymen who are desperate to see."

After nearly twenty hours of travel, we arrived at the airport in Yerevan, Armenia. Again, the customs officer was thoroughly puzzled about what to do with the box I was carrying. I assured him it contained corneas strictly for charitable, noncommercial transplants. I even showed officials a letter from California congresswoman Lois Capps stating her support of this SEE International mission. Still, the airport officials planned to confiscate the corneas and send them to the Ministry of Health for inspection and review.

While my two colleagues waited outside in a taxi, the customs officials sent me to their office. They set the box on a desk while they contemplated what to do with me and my hand-carried, well-packed cargo. As they pondered the situation, I stomped my feet in frustration, telling them that time was of the essence and my corneas must accompany me. As my agitation rose, so did my voice. "These are my corneas and if you take them, you must take me, too. If you put them in a freezer, you must put me in the freezer, too," I insisted.

To discuss this unprecedented situation, presumably without my input, they decided to have a meeting in private and left me alone in the waiting room outside their office. The box remained on the table. As soon as they closed the door, I jumped up, grabbed the box, and rushed outside. With my heart going into a tachycardia state, I dove into the taxi and ordered the driver to take off. I was relieved when he hit the gas and sped out of the airport. Drs. Ohanesian and Hill stared at me with eyes wide and eyebrows at attention, shocked by my daring act. I smiled slightly and responded more bravely than I felt, "This is my property. I wasn't going to leave it behind!"

The taxi driver took us directly to the hospital. We were all relieved when we reached our destination without further incident. I immediately

My last day working with the staff in Armenia. *Photo courtesy of Aisha Simjee*

went to the chief of staff's office and handed him the box for safekeeping. I relayed to him the situation that had occurred in customs and my concern that the officials would come to the hospital. He shrugged and smiled. "Let them come," he said. "I'll handle them." Fortunately, there were no repercussions. Still, I couldn't help looking over my shoulder, wondering if the authorities would come and arrest the foreign doctor for toting and absconding with body parts.

The next morning I began screening patients to determine who should receive the corneas. I found about fifty individuals who needed them. I wanted all of them to see but made the selection based on their corneal disease or infection, general eye health, and overall medical condition. Corneas with the highest endothelial counts, which have the highest potential for success, went to the younger patients.

Local ophthalmologist Alex Malayan, MD, headed the Republican Hospital's (now Malayan Eye Institute's) department of ophthalmology. He happened to be a cornea transplant surgeon and had a few patients who needed corneas. Dr. Malayan promised to check on all of the transplant patients after my departure. For the next six months he would have to follow up with them, since it takes six months for the cornea to completely heal following transplantation.

Although Dr. Malayan had the necessary surgical training, corneas and supplies were simply not available to him. As is true of everywhere I have gone with corneas, I offered to teach the local doctors how to remove corneas from corpses and refrigerate them in a nutrient media, in the hope that someone will take the initiative to pursue establishing an eye bank service. The lack of eye banks is compounded by pathetically poor public awareness about donating and, in many countries, regulatory roadblocks. Fortunately for Armenians, on subsequent trips, Dr. Ohanesian and other American doctors have helped them establish a corneal eye bank.

The local doctors were very excited to observe and participate in our surgeries. I wanted to spend more time with them but was frustrated by the limited working hours. Public transportation was so poor in the city that most hospital workers couldn't arrive before 10:00 a.m.; therefore, no surgeries started before 11:00 a.m. At the time of our visit, the country also suffered from a severe gasoline shortage. Petroleum trucks came infrequently to filling stations, where long lines of cars waited for a fill-up.

It was sad to see the widespread poverty, not only in material goods, but also in the spirit of the people. Many of their eyes were devoid of hope. Everyone who could was leaving the country and heading for other parts of the world. Armenia is the only country I have been where the population was decreasing each year, at least at the time of my visit.[1]

At one time in Yerevan, the biggest city in Armenia, beautiful trees lined the main street. When I was there, all that remained were stumps. The people had cut the trees down because they needed the wood to burn to warm their houses. Yet standing on that main road, I was awestruck by a national treasure dominating the skyline: majestic, snowcapped Mount Ararat. This seventeen-thousand-foot dormant volcano is considered by many scholars of the Bible and Qur'an to be the resting place of Noah's Ark[2] and today serves as a powerful symbol of the resilient Republic of Armenia.

After returning home, Dr. Ohanesian had Dr. Hill examine his mother-in-law and then decided to have Dr. Hill check his eyes as well. Dr. Hill diagnosed Dr. Ohanesian with occludable angles, a precursor to angle-closure glaucoma. Consequently, Dr. Ohanesian underwent a laser peripheral iridotomy (LPI) procedure to avoid this very serious condition that leads to rapid vision loss. His experience underscores the need for regular, routine eye exams, even in the absence of symptoms. I would liken their importance to regular mammograms for women, as early detection greatly improves the chances of successful treatment.

Dr. Ohanesian recently told me that in general, health conditions in Armenia have improved dramatically, crediting the character of the resident doctors who persevered during unbearably tough times. Soon after our trip, he organized a mobile eye hospital that travels to remote parts of Armenia to care for patients who don't have the transportation to seek out eye treatment. The mobile eye hospital, equipped with ophthalmic instrumentation and lasers, is used for eye exams and anterior segment surgeries, including cornea transplant, glaucoma, and cataract surgeries. Hundreds of thousands of socially vulnerable patients across Armenia have now received eye care through this hospital on wheels, and several times each year, American doctors visit and donate their time and services.

Dr. Ohanesian provided me with this update in June 2012:

> Armenia is now called an ophthalmology center of excellence by the ministers of health of several countries. All eye-care specialties are represented in this republic of

3 million people. Besides the presence of the two major eye hospitals, the mobile eye hospital is now in its fifth revolution around the country, treating rural residents at no charge. The mobile eye hospital has seen more than 350,000 patients and operated on 15,000 patients. It's an eighteen-wheel tractor-trailer with a five-hundred-kilowatt generator, making it self-contained. It has a separate heating and air conditioning system so that the surgeons may operate and patients may be examined in comfort.

The main hospital has retina, cornea, glaucoma, neuroophthalmology, orbital surgery, pediatrics, low vision, and eye banking specialty clinics. It also has an education center and surgical training wet lab.

In 2012, the Armenian EyeCare Project completed its twentieth year of activities. During that time, AECP sponsored several academic fellowships at US institutions for Armenian doctors. These fellowships provided yearlong training in retina, glaucoma, pediatrics, uveitis, cornea, eye banking, low vision, neuroophthalmology, and orbital surgery specialties, and additional fellowships are planned. Those who trained have gone on to establish training programs of their own in Armenia.

All these advances were possible because of the Armenian EyeCare Project and Dr. Ohanesian. He has been so successful in developing a screening and prevention program with laser and surgical treatment that other countries in the area are interested in acquiring the techniques that Armenia has learned.

With unwavering enthusiasm, Dr. Ohanesian went on to say,

In 2012, we are presenting our eleventh International Conference on Ophthalmology, which brings together attendees from Kazakhstan, Turkmenistan, Uzbekistan,

Ukraine, Georgia, and Turkey. They will discuss the disease of ROP [retinopathy of prematurity], which has been inadequately treated in these regions. This conference will include neonatologists, pediatricians, pediatric ophthalmologists, and retinal surgeons. It has the endorsement of the US State Department.

A regional occupational program has been endorsed by the United States ambassador as a center of excellence and has a nationwide screening and treatment program, including a surgical tier. The doctors in Armenia continue to be on the forefront of medicine, using their skill and determination to achieve excellence in their chosen fields. It has been a wonderful experience for all who have become involved with the project.

The same year that I went to Armenia, I ventured to two more Eastern European countries that had been severely impacted by revolutions leading to the end of communist rule. Romania and Bulgaria were my next destinations.

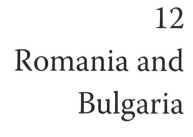

12
Romania and Bulgaria

The world is full of Kings and Queens,
Who blind your eyes and steal your dreams.
RONNIE JAMES DIO

In 1999, I was asked to go to both Romania and Bulgaria to deliver two donated lasers. I was elated to hear that SEE International pledged the YAG (yttrium-aluminum-garnet) laser machines to these struggling nations following recommendations from ophthalmologists who had visited them.

I invited ophthalmologist Arthur Charap, MD, to join me and assist with the machine assembly and surgical work. I have known Dr. Charap since he was in his residency at UCI, where I used to scrub in with the residents on surgical cases. I appreciated having him with me because he is an extremely intelligent ophthalmologist. He is nearly two feet taller than I am and outweighs me by at least one hundred pounds, and he never became upset when I dressed him down about his eyes frequently following pretty young ladies or when our hosts offered to treat us to a meal and he suggested we go to one of the area's best restaurants. "We shouldn't be acting like big shots," I remember scolding him. "It's not right of us to expect such treatment when our hosts probably don't have that kind of money. And when you order, don't ask for wine. Tea is less expensive."

Bucharest, Romania

That September, it took three planes and two days for us to arrive in Romania's largest city and capital, Bucharest. One of my most vivid memories of the people there was their love for red hair. It seemed as if anyone who could afford to do so dyed his or her locks. Unfortunately, many of the people were struggling just to survive due to political and economic turmoil. Poverty was rampant. We traveled to our destination on one-lane roads, where we would have to stop and wait for cars coming from the other direction. Romanian gypsies were everywhere along the roadside, selling produce and trinkets.

Dr. Charap and I were pleased to have a busy surgical schedule at the Clinical Eye Hospital of Bucharest. This was coordinated with the help of the hospital's chief of ophthalmology, Paul-Ioan Grecu, MD. With so many Romanians lacking access to eye care and thus in the advanced stages of their eye diseases, our services were in high demand. We could see that the YAG laser was going to be well utilized. In fact, in 2011, Dr. Charap heard from an ophthalmologist we had worked with there, Dr. Gabriella Murgoi, who told him the laser was still being used without any problems.

After completing our surgical work I went with a tour guide to see an architectural wonder, the massive and opulent Romanian parliament building. At that time the structure, known as the Palace of the Parliament, ranked as the second largest office building in the world (the first being the Pentagon in Arlington, Virginia). It stands today as a remarkable reminder of the excessive luxury in which former Romanian president Nicolae Ceauşescu would be living, had he survived. Marble walls, massive walnut doors, silk and velvet curtains, leather furniture, a glass dome, and a five-ton chandelier with seven thousand lights made it a sight to behold. The building was completed in 1989. But on December 25, 1989, the overthrown communist dictator and his wife were executed by firing squad, after years of robbing the country for personal gain.[1]

The grand, neoclassical architecture stood in stark contrast to what we observed outside. Leaving the building, I froze at the sight of destitute and deformed children camped at the footsteps of this building. Dozens of malnourished children with disabilities and missing limbs begged for money.

As we walked, I asked the tour guide, "Where are their parents?"

I was horrified to hear his bitter answer. "The megalomaniac Ceauşescu wanted to increase the population he ruled in Romania, so he had outlawed birth control and abortions, regardless of the status of the fetus. Even before he was executed, many of the children with disabilities were placed in orphanages that barely kept them alive and certainly did not provide adequate medical care or nourishment."

In my opinion, the obvious suffering in this place clearly showed the importance of abstinence, birth control, sex education, and good prenatal care. No one should bring children into the world when they cannot be cared for properly or given to someone who can look after their needs. If I were a developing nation's "queen for the day," my priority would be to ensure that the citizens had knowledge of and access to birth control.

Before every one of my trips, my husband and family urge me not to bring home any children. No matter where I have gone, I have seen children badly in need of help, especially disabled children. I pride myself on my stoicism, but at times like this I've given it up in the nearest restroom, where no one can see me crying.

Sofia, Bulgaria

After a short flight from Romania, we landed in Sofia, Bulgaria, for a three-day visit. We were met by the country's director of the International

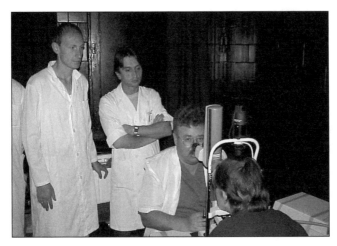

Bulgarian doctors become acquainted with their new laser. *Photo by Aisha Simjee*

Eye Foundation, Professor Petja Vassileva, MD, PhD, DSci, MPH. The wife of a wealthy businessman, she was also a distinguished physician and gracious woman working for low or no pay in a hospital where funding was sorely lacking. Prof. Vassileva's labors have reduced the prevalence of blindness and sight-impairing diseases in Bulgaria, and she has published hundreds of scientific articles over the years. She is credited with creating the first Bulgarian eye bank, among many other achievements, culminating in her subsequently being named Bulgaria's Physician of the Year in 2003.[2] Having earned her master's in public health from Johns Hopkins Bloomberg School of Public Health, Dr. Vassileva spoke excellent English.

Soon after we arrived, Professor Vassileva informed us, "You will be volunteering at Saint Anna University Hospital in the Pashev Center for Sight. At this time they aren't allowing elective surgeries."

I was puzzled. "Why would they place elective surgeries on hold?"

She sighed. "I'm sad to say that in its present circumstances, Bulgaria has become 'the toilet of Europe.'"

Bulgaria's economic crisis had resulted in high unemployment, reduced government revenue, and, thus, a poor health infrastructure.

The hospital simply didn't have the resources required for elective surgery and had run short of supplies.

A decade prior to my visit, with the disintegration of the Communist Bloc, Bulgaria's political and economic situation changed for the worse. The country was experiencing the second highest unemployment rate in Europe at 16 percent. By the late 1990s, half the population lived in poverty. Public social benefits had also declined and with economic deterioration came deterioration in healthcare.

In November, two months after my visit, then-president Bill Clinton became the first United States president to visit Bulgaria, marking the ten-year anniversary of the fall of communism and urging Bulgarians to "stay the course" on democratic reform, in spite of the economic problems of adapting to it. Subsequently, Bulgaria's economy has seen marked improvements.[3]

When Dr. Charap and I put the country's first YAG laser machine together and demonstrated its use, it thrilled the young local doctors and residents. I felt as if we had given them a beacon of hope. Because we brought with us the necessary surgical supplies, we were able to do a few surgeries in Sofia. Still, most of our time was spent showing the doctors and clinicians how to use the laser. Professor Vassileva was never far away, always making the necessary introductions and ensuring we were well fed.

In the years that followed my visit, Professor Vassileva has worked hard to bring a full clinical and surgical ophthalmic service to her country. In 2005, she helped arrange a Cyber-Sight telemedicine partnership between Saint Anna University Hospital in Sofia and ORBIS. This Internet-based program provides resources for ophthalmic medical education and consultations by expert mentors who are ORBIS International volunteer physicians.

As Dr. Charap and I flew back to the States, we reflected on our relief to be headed back to the comfort of our homes. We smiled to think about the men and women who would be rejoicing to regain their vision, especially now that the YAG laser enabled the clinicians to provide the standard of surgical ophthalmology. That reality made our efforts especially worthwhile. Within a year, Dr. Charap and I took another Eastern Europe medical mission, this time to Bosnia.

13
Bosnia

An eye for an eye,
and the whole world would be blind.
KAHLIL GIBRAN

M y daughter Sufia had always listened with rapt attention to my accounts of medical missions and, like her sister, would often tell me she wanted to come along and help. I felt that seeing the desperate conditions so prevalent yet foreign to most Americans would be eye-opening for a teenager born and raised in prosperous Orange County, as it had been for her sister. In 2000, while she was on summer break between her junior and senior year at Stanford University, she finally had the opportunity to accompany me. We headed for central Bosnia, with Dr. Charap also joining us for the trip.

"The war may be officially over, but bombs are still going off," Dr. Brown cautioned when I repeatedly called SEE asking for supplies for the trip. He finally relented. "SEE isn't officially supporting this trip," he made clear, "but I know I'm not going to change your mind about going."

After flying into the capital city of Sarajevo, we drove about forty-five miles to the town of Zenica, situated on the Bosna River, from which the country derives its name. The picturesque town is surrounded by mountains and hills. The peaceful scene belied the country's reputation

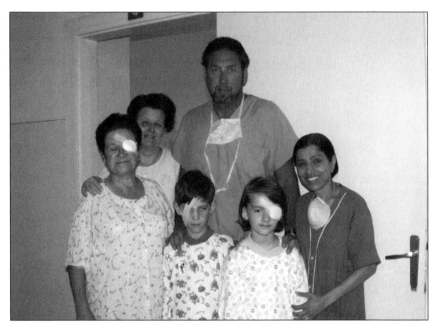

Dr. Arthur Charap and I with our patients following surgeries for cataract removal and traumatic injury repair. *Photo courtesy of Aisha Simjee*

as "the powder keg of Europe" for the many wars begun here and the unfortunate circumstances of its people, who lacked money for their basic human needs, not to mention the materials, facilities, and medical training to deliver and receive medical care. We saw numerous patients with opaque eyes from traumatic cataracts stemming from Bosnia's civil war, which ended in 1995.

Sufia, who has always been outgoing, enjoyed helping with the preop screenings and chatting with the hospital personnel and patients. One of the young nurses told Sufia how fortunate she was to go outside her country and see another part of the world. I felt these encounters were, for her, the best part of the trip. After living her entire life in California as the daughter of a doctor and a hospital administrator, she had her eyes opened to living without the surpluses and health services we Americans tend to take for granted. She left with a much greater appreciation for the challenges the poor face in meeting even their most basic physical needs. I felt the few thousand dollars I spent taking her on this trip was a better investment than the money I was spending on her Stanford education. As a student of the Bloomberg School of Public Health, Johns Hopkins University, Sufia subsequently spent several years in Nairobi, Kenya, working on her thesis concerning public health policy on contagious diseases in developing countries.

In spite of Bosnia's struggles, the people were very hospitable. Our hostess, Dr. Alma Cerim-Delic, and other medical team members took us to area restaurants to try the local food, all at their expense. The hospital, Kantonalna Bolnica, however, was poorly equipped. When I discovered that it did not have an operating ophthalmic microscope to do microsurgery, I placed a call to SEE International.

"I'd like to leave the portable microscope that you sent with me," I told the administrator. "I know the local ophthalmologists will put it to good use." SEE officials agreed to donate the instrument, and the local ophthalmologists were all smiles when I left the microscope with them.

After cataract surgeries were performed on several dozen patients, Sufia, Dr. Charap, and I took time to visit a refugee camp outside Zenica. On the way there we traveled through the hills lined with white tombstones as far as our eyes could see. It was a graphic representation of just how many people had been killed in the 1990s war between the Serbs and Croatians that left the country devastated.[1] Bosnia's poor sanitation systems, prevalent malnutrition in adults and children, high mortality rates, and lingering trauma from widespread physical and sexual violence were sobering reminders of the scars left by ethnic conflicts and war.

In a refugee camp outside of town we made friends with children who clustered around us as we passed out chewing gum, dried fruit, and candy. One barefoot, red-haired moppet named Sulemania who was no more than seven years of age had lost her parents and was living in the camp with her grandmother. My heart melted as she wrapped her tiny arms around me in a moment of happiness amid a bleak existence. Thousands of people were too afraid to go back to their homes because those who committed atrocities against their families were still there.

A bright spot of this trip was finding that many of the practicing ophthalmologists in Bosnia were women. I didn't expect this since Bosnia has a patriarchal society, influenced by both Eastern European and Islamic traditions, in which women are generally considered subservient to men. And yet, as stated by Nobel Peace Prize winner Kofi Annan, who at that time was the secretary-general of the United Nations, "Gender equality is critical to the development and peace of every nation."[2] Annan spread the message that no tool for development is more effective than the empowerment of women. I fully agree with his stance that when women thrive, all of society benefits, and succeeding generations are given a better start in life.

14
Philippines

There are many things we do not want about the world. Let us not just mourn them. Let us change them.

FERDINAND MARCOS

In the tropical Philippines, the dry season is from October to May, with monsoon season following from June to October. I planned my trip accordingly and arrived in April 2001. The manufacturer of phaco ultrasound machines, devices used in modern cataract surgery, sent one just before our arrival so that we could demonstrate its use for local doctors.

The trip was organized through a group of Filipino doctors that included Eduardita "Lani" Quevedo, MD, a Glendale, California, ophthalmologist hailing from and trained in the Philippines. Dr. Quevedo has a remarkable family history, which she shared while seated next to me on the flight. At one time her family held a place in the *Guinness Book of World Records* for their unprecedented number of medical professionals. Her father, who was a medical doctor, and her mother, an ophthalmic nurse, had nine children, and all nine became doctors—including two ophthalmologists. One was a practicing pediatric ophthalmologist in Cebu City, and during my ten days in the Philippines she welcomed me into her family's home.

We flew to the beautiful Philippines archipelago, a ring of islands. Coastal Cebu City is located on the main island of Cebu Province in the southern Philippines. Overall the people seemed to be happy, fulfilled, and thriving. I noticed that even children dressed in rags all seemed to have cell phones—a phenomenon that was not yet widespread in the United States at the turn of the century. The children were also already well versed at texting.

I worked in the Cebu City Medical Center, a large, government-subsidized hospital, and at the Cebu Doctors' Hospital, a private, paying hospital. Overall, Cebu City had a good number of well-qualified ophthalmologists servicing the local people. It was, of all the places I have visited, the one where I felt least needed. Nevertheless, the physicians and hospital staff relished having me demonstrate phacoemulsification cataract surgery with the phaco machine delivered by the manufacturer to the hospital. They observed how, through a tiny incision, the needle of this ultrasonic device breaks the lens into pieces and sucks them out of the eye so that the cloudy lens can be replaced with a new, artificial lens. Previously, a surgeon would make a wider incision on the side of the cornea and remove the core of the lens in one piece and the rest of the lens by suction.

At that time, this large general hospital's operating room had only nine nurses, including the head nurse doing the administrative work. Of the remaining eight, only one or two were familiar with eye surgery. Most of the cleaning, sterilizing, pre- and postoperative area care, patient transport, and supply inventory tasks were handled by residents.

One of the local nurses I met while in the OR told me he was going to New Jersey to work there in a hospital. I quickly did the math. That would leave just seven OR nurses at this 300-bed hospital.

Across the street from the hospital was a nursing school. Hospital recruiters from the United States, Germany, England, and the Middle East were frequent visitors to their school, offering scholarships to help students finish their schooling and assistance with passing the required nursing exams and acquiring immigrant or working visas.

By design and with the support of the government, the Philippines had become the leading source country for nurses internationally. An estimated 85 percent of employed Filipino nurses work internationally, leaving thousands of unfilled nursing positions in the Philippines.[1]

I hoped to take a couple of days before leaving this island nation to see the countryside and coastline of the capital city, Manila. However, on my way back to Manila, where I would catch my flight back to the States, the local authorities advised me that it would be best to leave due to volatile political unrest.[2] In January 2001, just three months prior to my visit, President Joseph Estrada was ousted and later arrested for plundering millions from state funds. This led to protests by the people, an attack on the presidential palace, and firefights that killed soldiers and civilians alike. While the country declared a "state of rebellion" until public order could be restored, I took the authorities' advice and flew straight home.

15
New York: Post-9/11

If we learn nothing else from this
tragedy, we learn that life is short
and there is no time for hate.

SANDY DAHL

While preparing to leave for work I heard the morning news that not one but two planes had flown into the World Trade Center. The shock of knowing our country had been attacked was coupled with my concern for the lives affected, in particular my sponsored daughter and niece, Nasima H. Simjee, who had been working in the South Tower, ninety-sixth floor.

My daughters—Alia in Philadelphia, Pennsylvania, and Sufia in Washington, DC—immediately prepared to go to New York to look for Nasima. Following the advice of local officials, they scoured area hospitals and makeshift morgues in search of her remains. In the end, the closest they came was the discovery of a partially burned identification badge of one of her known coworkers and the burned-up ID card of her supervisor, with only the name still legible.

Just a few years earlier, Nasima's mother, my sister Rabia, had made her way to America and was living with her family in Orange, California. I spoke with Rabia by phone several times over the next few days, offering what comfort I could. When she and my niece Salma expressed a desire to go to New York to look for Nasima, I didn't hesitate to say I would join them.

At the end of September we flew in and boarded New York's Port Authority ferry to head across the Hudson River to Ground Zero. A gray dust seemed to cover lower Manhattan, and the smell of burned chemicals and smoke and quite possibly decaying human remains lingered in the air. Everywhere I looked there were police cars, fire trucks, ambulances, and military vehicles, and virtually all the civilian vehicles I saw flew American flags from their windows. A newly erected tent city was a sea of somber humanity. Family members desperately hoped that their loved ones had survived and emerged from the rubble. Everyone we encountered seemed to share a bond so that we were no longer strangers but rather brokenhearted patriots with a new appreciation for our country and all we held dear.

Salma, like me, tends to be stoic, even in the worst of times. Rabia could not contain her grief during the days as we searched and even less so in the evenings as we stayed in Nasima's neatly kept apartment on Sixty-Seventh Street, near Broadway and Columbus Avenues. Nasima's needlepoint embroidery proudly displayed on her walls was an endearing reminder of the industrious and innocent young woman who was lost to us.

To comfort my older sister, I declared, "To honor Nasima, I will do what I can to help those who suffer." In Nasima's name, I was recommitting myself to using my time, talents, and treasure for the benefit of those who are hurting. It was my way of turning my anger and grief into energy that would lead to healing for me, my family, and people everywhere. I believe Rabia took solace as she saw me delivering on that promise, but five years to the day later, on September 11, 2006, we buried her. Understandably, she never quite recovered from such a devastating, senseless loss.

Ten years later, I returned to Ground Zero with Sabi, Alia, Sufia, and Salma for ceremonies to commemorate the anniversary of our country's darkest hour. With reverence, we visited the memorial pool at the World Trade Center site and traced our fingers over the "S41" bronze plaque where Nasima's name is inscribed, which we found among nearly three thousand others representing victims from ninety-three countries.

Throughout the day we, along with thousands of others closely affected by the events of 9/11, heard from President Barack Obama, former president George W. Bush, Mayor Michael Bloomberg, former mayor Rudy Giuliani, Secretary of State Hillary Clinton, and Governor Andrew Cuomo. But when I recall the anniversary events, what I remember most is not the speeches, as meaningful as they were, but the women as well as some men surrounding me who were unashamedly weeping. In fact, Sabi became somewhat irritated with me for not remaining still and listening but rather scurrying to get cups of water to help quell the sobs of complete strangers in our midst.

Since our country was rocked by 9/11, I have done my best to keep the promise I made to Rabia by serving in my community and undertaking medical missions to another thirteen developing nations. The terrorists did not win, and Nasima did not die in vain.

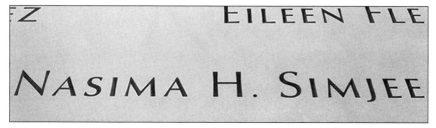

Seeing Nasima's name along with hundreds of other innocent victims' names inscribed on the 9/11 Memorial brought up a range of emotions for me: sadness at our loss, anger over the atrocity, solidarity with my countrymen, pride in our nation, and by having labored for others in Nasima's name, a sense of peace and healing. *Photo by Aisha Simjee*

16
Nepal

*The purpose of life is
a life of purpose.*
ROBERT BYRNE

According to the World Health Organization, cataracts account for
67 percent of blindness in the Nepalese people,[1] despite existing
technology that can restore vision at an extremely low cost. Reducing
the backlog of cataract blindness directly addresses poverty. It requires
training ophthalmic personnel, strengthening the existing healthcare
infrastructure, and making care affordable and surgical supplies available.
I was impressed by the strides Nepal was making in these areas, although
the task remains monumental.

Located in the Himalayas of South Asia between India and China,
Nepal is home to nearly 29 million people, with about 40 percent living
in poverty,[2] and few physicians to care for the masses. One in twenty-
three Nepalese suffers from cataracts and thirty-three out of every one
thousand people suffer from other sorts of eye diseases.[3] In the far-flung
regions of this nation, many of the Nepalese do not even know that a
cure is possible.

I had planned to travel solo in 2002 to visit a village at the foot
of Mount Everest, the highest point on Earth. But my plans changed

days before departure when I was informed of a malaria outbreak at my destination. WHO strongly advised visitors not to go to that village.

Not wanting to waste my travel arrangements or the time I had committed to the Nepalese people, I immediately began planning how to salvage my mission. After discussing the situation with staff from SEE International, B. P. Koirala Lions Centre for Ophthalmic Studies in Kathmandu became my destination.

Kathmandu, the capital and largest city of Nepal, is heavily urbanized and still has a prevalent caste system. This system excludes lower caste groups from land ownership and limits people in these groups to jobs considered menial, degrading, or dirty. Because of the religious beliefs in Kathmandu, where many are Hindus, it is hard to drive, even in downtown Kathmandu, without stopping for meandering cattle, which many of the locals consider sacred. This country's practice of child labor was particularly disturbing to me. I recall watching an eight-year-old girl cooking over an open fire, worrying that she would be burned. Although in 2000 the Nepali government abolished the bonded labor system, the practice still exists.

In contrast to the social injustices and grim poverty, this tiny country possesses natural beauty in abundance. At the end of my trip, I ventured just outside the city to a small airport and boarded a sixteen-passenger plane for some extremely satisfying sightseeing. About one hundred miles from Kathmandu in the Himalayan mountain range, I was awestruck by the bird's-eye view of majestic Mount Everest, the world's highest mountain at 29,029 feet. Upon my colleague's advice I also visited Shivapuri National Park. Located in the Kathmandu Valley, the park features thick vegetation of pines, oaks, rhododendrons, and tropical trees surrounded by mountains. Tourists come to hear their echo when they call out.

Of greater interest to me, however, was the B. P. Koirala Lions Centre for Ophthalmic Studies, based in Kathmandu. It operates as a collaborative project with Tribhuvan University, Nepal's largest public medical school, and as part of Tribhuvan University Hospital, the country's largest hospital and growing at 444 beds in 2011. This training hospital was open to anyone, regardless of his or her economic standing.

One of the faces that haunts me from my visit is that of a young mother whose left eye and thus her pretty face had been decimated by an advanced squamous cell carcinoma. While Americans have been repeatedly told that catching a disease in its earliest stages provides the best chance for recovery and survival, this truth is not widely known or accepted in many cultures, such as hers. Another incorrect belief is "When hair turns white, then the eye turns white; then you will die." In modern society it's been proven that although cataracts often come with age and turn the lens white, they are highly curable.

Most of my time at the center was spent working with three very motivated senior residents from other countries of Southeast Asia. The female physician was Bhutanese and the two males were Cambodian. In their own countries, eye surgery training programs were available. They had studied ophthalmology in their homelands and planned to return and work there. But first, these ambitious residents wanted to broaden their horizons by learning in neighboring countries where eye programs were perceived to be more advanced and modern technology was available. In my visit to the nearby medical school, I was pleasantly surprised to see many more female students.

Years later in the hallways of Aravind Eye Hospital in India on a visit to observe high-volume cataract surgeries, I ran into the slender Bhutanese doctor who had been a resident in Kathmandu. "I remember you!" she declared with delight.

"I am so pleased to see you again and to see how committed you are to advancing your knowledge!" I exclaimed.

"Yes, and what about you?" she countered. "You, too, are going throughout Asia to learn what's being done. You are just as enthusiastic as I am!" We hope she can come to the United States and visit me in

Orange at St. Joseph Hospital someday, and she invited me to visit her once she is established in her local hospital.

I brought three corneas to Nepal, and we performed several cataract surgeries. In Koirala Eye Hospital, most of the cataract surgeries were done using the manual small incision cataract surgery technique known as MSICS. It's a newer, better surgery than routine extracapsular cataract extraction (ECCE), albeit more technically difficult.

At that time, the eye hospital did not yet have a phaco machine for cataract surgery. In wealthier countries, ECCE has been replaced by phacoemulsification, which has been shown to achieve quicker recoveries and superior outcomes. However, a new phaco machine costs in the neighborhood of $60,000, and it is still a rarity in developing countries.

I was a little surprised to discover that the Koirala clinic was relatively well equipped in comparison to other hospitals in that region and those I've seen in capital cities in other countries. Founder Bisheshwar Prasad (B. P.) Koirala's philosophy was that sight is a paramount asset for a country as poor as Nepal. He successfully argued that enabling its citizens to see and thereby work and feed themselves as contributing members of society was a top priority.

The late B. P. Koirala was once the prime minister of Nepal. In a 2010 speech memorializing him, assistant secretary-general of the United Nations Kul Chandra Gautam said B. P. would have "felt very proud of what the [B. P. Koirala Eye] Foundation is doing in terms of research, advocacy and program implementation to promote access to eye care especially among women and children, and to reduce inequity in health and education services for our country's under-privileged communities."[4]

During my visit, I was also fortunate to meet Dr. Koirala's son, Shashank Koirala, MD, who was serving as a professor at the B. P. Koirala Lions Centre for Ophthalmic Studies. Nepal remains one of the poorest countries in the world, but richer for having this visionary family restoring sight for thousands of countrymen.

17
Afghanistan

*There are three classes of people:
Those who see. Those who see when
they are shown. Those who do not see.*

LEONARDO DA VINCI

On August 6, 2010, an International Assistance Mission (IAM) team of ten unarmed doctors, nurses, and logistics personnel providing badly needed eye treatments in northern Afghanistan were ambushed, robbed, and slaughtered.[1] When I read the news reported by the Associated Press, it hit me hard. A year earlier I was welcomed to Afghanistan by IAM and worked with the team leader, Dr. Tom Little, an optometrist from New York and father of three children who had served for thirty-three years in Afghanistan. A certificate of appreciation given to me by Dr. Little hangs in my office hallway. One of his closest family members is a patient of mine.

The IAM team of six Americans, one German, one Briton, and two Afghan interpreters was on a humanitarian trip to the Nuristan Province, where they had treated about four hundred people in remote villages suffering from various illnesses. Among the team was Dr. Karen Woo, a young family practitioner from London engaged to be married. Before embarking on the trip, she blogged about her plans. Dubbing herself "Explorer Kitten," she wrote, "The trek will not be easy; it will take three

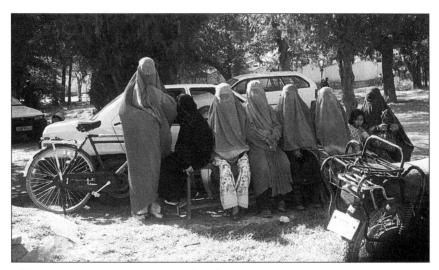

Afghani women await treatment. *Photo by Aisha Simjee*

weeks and be done on foot and with packhorses—no vehicles can access the mountainous terrain . . . The expedition will require a lot of physical and mental resolve and will not be without risk but ultimately, I believe that the provision of medical treatment is of fundamental importance and that the effort is worth it in order to assist those that need it most."[2]

Most of the Afghanis love Americans and are very grateful for the help we provide. While the villagers do not have the means to read what Dr. Woo naively wrote, there is a strong likelihood that others with bad intent used her blog to find the team and carry out these senseless killings.

When I travel to places such as Afghanistan, I never talk about my plans, and while I am there, I never flaunt the fact that I am a doctor. I put on a scarf, I go to the hospital, and I find a reliable person to take me to and from my lodgings. I have the advantage of being small and dark and can easily blend in.

According to a Taliban spokesman, the IAM team was gunned down because they were "spying for the Americans" and "preaching

Christianity." That is absolute nonsense. Having worked with IAM, I know that they were not spies and were not out proselytizing. This was sheer stupidity, setting back the work that has helped thousands of suffering Afghanis.

Dr. Tom, as people there called him, oversaw eye hospitals in Kabul and two other cities, as well as a few clinics in smaller towns. One of those hospitals, University Eye Hospital, was part of Kabul Medical University. During my 2009 visit to Afghanistan, I had worked there and donated ophthalmology devices. The hospital later closed due to a lack of funding and much of the equipment was taken, but IAM stepped in to run it. As part of Dr. Tom's work in the training of eye doctors there, he served as negotiator with the Ministry of Higher Education to advance clinical training.

I have taken two medical mission trips to Kabul, Afghanistan. The first time was in September 2002, exactly one year after 9/11, and the second time was in May 2009. While in most places one could expect to see progress after seven years, I saw more damaged roads and broken buildings everywhere, as well as worse traffic.

On a positive note, in conjunction with the Ministry of Higher Education, United States aid has funded the construction or refurbishment of more than 680 schools throughout Afghanistan since 2002.[3] During my first visit, I attended an opening ceremony of a middle school for girls, which was built by American soldiers. I also observed that conditions in the eye hospitals had improved significantly, with better equipment and facilities.

For my trip in 2002 I contacted several nonprofit, nongovernmental organizations (NPOs/NGOs) to see if one of them could help me out on the receiving side. Hope *Worldwide*[4], a London-based organization, and Dr. Mark Timlin, founder of Hope *Worldwide* Afghanistan and family practitioner, stepped up.

As with most of my flights, as I boarded the plane to Afghanistan, I went to see and shake hands with the airplane crew members, and

Visiting Afghanistan's deputy minister of public health, Dr. Nadera Burhani. On the wall hangs a portrait of Afghanistan President Hamid Karzai. *Photo courtesy of Aisha Simjee*

with a big smile told them I was an ophthalmologist carrying a box of corneas and asked to use their refrigerator. The corneas are packed in the smallest foam box I can find, and refrigeration helps preserve them as long as possible.

Along with cornea transplants, I treated patients suffering from scars on the eyelids related to leishmaniasis, a painful parasitic disease that results from the bite of sand flies on exposed parts of the body. It is rarely seen in the United States but is common in some parts of the world, including Afghanistan. When the bug dies, it leaves a lesion that eventually becomes a scar, and when the scar is close to the eyelid, it can result in deformities that must be surgically corrected.

Leishmaniasis was treated there by injecting medicine via a large syringe next to the lesion to kill the bugs and render the lesion inactive. As many as twenty-five injections may be needed by one individual, depending on his or her condition. Most lesions occur on the face and

Children
attend the
opening
celebration
for their
new school,
built by
American
soldiers.
*Photos by
Aisha Simjee*

exposed parts of the body, such as the hands and feet, and the condition will not resolve without medical treatment.

WHO representative to Afghanistan Peter Graaf said that leishmaniasis had affected more than sixty-five thousand people in Kabul.[5] "This number is likely to be the tip of the iceberg as cases are grossly underreported owing to poor diagnostic tools and the stigma that is attached to this disease," he stated.

I visited a Kabul clinic run by WHO, Karte Seh Hospital, along with Wazir Akbar Khan Hospital, where children were being treated for the disease. Many were screaming and had to be held down to receive the injections without local anesthesia. Some children were cold and clammy, a worrisome indication that they might be going into shock. After about four hours, I couldn't take it anymore and had to leave.

While in Kabul, I also went to the Indira Gandhi Children's Hospital, which was brimming with sick children. Doctors and staff primarily from India ran the hospital. Because of the overcrowded conditions, I was not able to see any eye patients since no examination rooms were available other than those needed to see sick children. Only basic, urgent care could be provided at that time.

The local doctors in Afghanistan hail from several of the area's local tribes. The Pashtuns are the largest tribe and generally have the highest social standing. The people from northeast Afghanistan, from the Hazara tribe, have features similar to those of the neighboring Mongolians and are considered an inferior class by other tribes. I couldn't care less about people's lineage and the rungs of the social scale. In fact, I spent a good deal of time training a young Hazara second-year resident. He wasn't used to so much attention, and when I left he fought back tears.

During this first visit, I stayed in the second-story home of Hope *Worldwide* Afghanistan founder Dr. Mark Timlin and his Australian wife, Vicky—a hardworking couple if there ever was one. With her red hair, light complexion, and blue eyes, Vicky looked conspicuous in public,

This child's white pupil clearly exhibits retinoblastoma, a rare, cancerous tumor of the retina. Her mother suffered from the same condition in her hidden right eye. *Photo by Aisha Simjee*

even though she covered herself with a hijab. I was a light sleeper and once, in the middle of the night, I heard what sounded like bombing. I quickly grabbed my scarf and purse. Mark knocked on my door and said we should go outside. He went out first to evaluate the situation, and we joined others from neighboring houses gathering on the street. They determined it had been a bomb blast close by, but we were safe and could go back inside.

The Timlins talked with me about wanting children, but they were hesitant to move forward because of the conditions of their environment. Still, I encouraged them to do so. Soon after, they went back to Australia and started a family. Their firstborn child was a girl, whom they named Aisha.

For my second trip to Afghanistan in 2009, I traveled with a heavy load of supplies. The extra weight cost me $1,350, which Emirates Airlines promised to return to me but never did. My boxes included a slit lamp, used but in excellent condition; punctal plugs for dry eyes; surgical instruments; loops; glasses collected in my office that were donated by my patients; antibiotics; glaucoma medications; steroid drops; sutures; Ahmed valves for glaucoma procedures; nonsteroidal anti-inflammatory drug (NSAID) drops; and amniotic membranes.

As soon as I arrived at my destination, I screened the patients, who had been waiting for hours or even days to be seen, and performed surgeries. This time I brought twelve corneas, but we could have used ten times as many.

At University Eye Hospital (unfortunately now closed due to a lack of funding), I was able to train local doctors in the harvesting and preservation of corneas taken from corpses. I performed cornea transplants on two children and three women, and the rest of the corneas were given to local doctors to use. For each patient, I always operate on just one eye—the worse eye—thereby helping as many people as possible. The women were ages twenty-seven to fifty-five, the latter being older than most patients I would treat. But the fifty-five-year-old told me she needed to see to take care of her grandchildren.

At the end of my second trip to Kabul, I went to visit Nadera Burhani, deputy minister of public health. I was accompanied by Dr. Waheed Hafizi from Noor Eye Hospital. It was not easy for us to see Dr. Burhani since we went to her office without an appointment. The doorkeeper–security guard was not planning to allow us in until he found out I was an ophthalmologist. He asked me if I would see his mother, which I did later that day, although her condition required a neurosurgeon to remove a tumor behind the eye.

We were granted five minutes with Dr. Burhani, but Dr. Hafizi and I ultimately spent about twenty minutes talking. I showed her the empty box in which I had carried the corneas from the United States and explained to her how I brought them into the country. We talked about the fact that the local doctors had to get corneas from eye banks

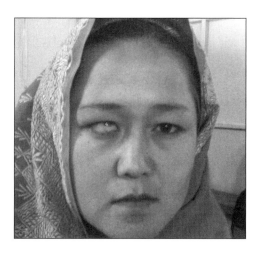

This young Afghani woman asked that I fix her eye because, she said, she wanted to find a husband. *Photo courtesy of Aisha Simjee*

in Germany and Czechoslovakia. These corneas were very expensive, and almost no one could afford them.

I pointed out to her that next door to University Eye Hospital was a mortuary. "How," I asked, "in good conscience could a community ask someone from out of the country to donate eyes from their eye bank, when people in the local community do not donate their own eyes? After harvesting the corneas, the corpses' eyes can be sewn shut, so no one can even tell the corneas have been removed. Is that too much to ask? Couldn't families be persuaded to give permission to donate the corneas from their late relatives? Money to start an eye bank should not be a major issue, because it's simply a matter of doing some basic blood tests on the donor and keeping the corneas in a nutrient media in the refrigerator. I'm willing to buy the refrigerator and send the media bottles."

Although Dr. Burhani was impressed with my presentation, thanked me profusely for my work, and wished me well, she did not make any commitments. It would be wonderful to hear that the community opened a local eye bank, but I would be surprised if that happened.

I have made arrangements to donate my eyes when I die, even though I will be old and the cell count will not be high enough for transplantation. At least they can be removed and used for training purposes.

Meeting the health needs in Afghanistan will continue to be a monumental challenge. The people's best chance is to learn to take care of each other. As soon as I heard of the tragic killings in August 2010, I contacted Dr. Hafizi, offering my condolences and a return visit to Afghanistan. With the permission of the local health ministry, I hope to be back one day. And if I can go, I plan to spend all my time training local doctors in the medical and surgical treatment of eye conditions so that they can carry on the good work done by Dr. Tom Little.

18
Panama

Kindness is a language which
the deaf can hear and
the blind can see.

MARK TWAIN

S EE International invited me to work in Panama in 2003. SEE had
been contacted by Ruben Orillac, MD, who initiated the first SEE
International surgery clinics in Panama in 1985. Dr. Orillac is well
educated, up-to-date in ophthalmology, and speaks excellent English.
I knew of Dr. Orillac from his attendance at meetings of the American
Academy of Ophthalmology (AAO) and Pan-American Association of
Ophthalmology. At the time of my visit, he chaired the Panamanian
Ophthalmology Society.

Dr. Orillac informed SEE that he was collaborating with a branch of
Lions Club International, and they were ready to receive an ophthalmic
surgeon to assist him and his associates in taking care of a heavy load of
cataract patients. He assured SEE that follow-up on cases done by SEE
ophthalmologists would not be a problem, since his office was within
walking distance of where we would be operating for the Lions Club.

I happily accepted the invitation to Panama and arranged my traveling
papers. But I nearly cancelled my trip just a few days before I was scheduled
to leave, which just doesn't happen once I've made up my mind.

My daughter Alia had become seriously ill with severe abdominal pain from gastrointestinal inflammation. I called and told my host I didn't feel I should go, but the doctor was earnestly convincing.

"Please come," cajoled Dr. Orillac. "Perhaps you could limit your trip time, but it would be such an ordeal to cancel so many patients."

Alia heard me fielding phone calls and knew that months of work had gone into arranging the visit. Looking pale but putting on a brave smile, she encouraged me to go as planned. "Dad and my cousins will see that I'm well taken care of," she assured me. I knew her condition was well managed by capable physicians and family; nevertheless, I trimmed my trip plans from two weeks to eight days—two days for travel and six days for treating patients.

With my daughter entrusted to the capable hands of my husband and sister, I flew solo to Miami and on to Panama City. I arrived around midnight and slept for a few hours in a room offered by Dr. and Mrs. Orillac. This tall, lovely couple welcomed me to their elegant condominium, twenty or so floors above Panama City Beach. It blended with the high-rise apartment buildings and condos, office complexes, and hotels forming the sparkling, picture-perfect Panama City skyline. How luxurious and refreshing my lodging was when compared to my accommodations in countries where I worked and slept on the floor!

The Orillacs graciously offered to take me out for dinner, but I politely refused. "I'd really prefer to have whatever your housekeeper can come up with. I want to focus all my time and energy on our patients first thing in the morning," I explained.

Early the next day, Mrs. Orillac, impeccably groomed in a professional pantsuit, gave me a ride to the clinic. The facility was an outpatient surgery center with a sign in front bearing the Lions Club International name and insignia. Lions' sight projects worldwide have prevented serious vision loss for millions, including 7 million patients receiving cataract surgeries. I've also had the privilege of working with the organization in Africa and Cambodia.

We entered the clinic to find Spanish-speaking patients of mixed American Indian, African, and European ancestry lined up and filling all the waiting-room chairs. I started my preop checkups and listed those who were candidates for surgery for that afternoon. Everything was free for the patients, including services donated by nursing staff. While these people had no regular healthcare, they were not as hopelessly poverty-stricken as people I had seen in other parts of the world. They were relatively clean and had homes in which to recover.

That week the clinic was open exclusively to four ophthalmologists, including Dr. Orillac and me, along with support staff to treat patients with no means to pay for needed surgical services. The other two ophthalmologists, both local male doctors, were delighted to see my suitcase's stock of supplies for cataract and extraocular (eye muscle) surgeries.

The operating room staff was extremely well trained and very familiar with ophthalmological processes. The ophthalmologists were especially interested in the soft, foldable acrylic lenses that I showed them. The burrito-type fold makes the implant easier to insert through a smaller incision than the standard hard polymethyl methacrylate posterior chamber implants they had been using. When I brought the implants and demonstrated their insertion, they were still cost prohibitive, but foldable implants have since become the standard of care in many parts of the world.

In spite of my restricted schedule, near the end of my time in Panama, the Orillacs took me on a tour of their town. In a couple of hours I saw several ocean fish farms and, close to them, the Panama Canal. Lots of tourists were on hand to check out this historic crossroads, but I have to admit it reminded me of boats going through a parking lot with a gate.

The famous Panama ship canal joins the Atlantic and Pacific Oceans, passing through the land bridge between North and South America. I was fascinated to learn that in the 1500s, Panama became the crossroads and marketplace of Spain's empire in the New World. In 1903, with support from the United States, Panama proclaimed its independence. Panama signed a treaty calling for the United States to build a canal and defend it. In 1914, the United States completed what is still considered one of the world's greatest engineering feats.[1]

A domestic political crisis and an attack on the United States embassy in Panama in 1987 led to a freeze on US economic assistance. In 1989, President George H.W. Bush ordered the United States military into Panama to protect US lives and property and to defend its treaty responsibility to operate and defend the canal. In 1999, command of the waterway was given to the Panamanian government. Today, Panama enjoys one of the most positive economic growth rates in Central America.[2]

No doubt many Panamanians are multilingual, yet I was surprised to find that, as close as Panama is to US territories, very few people I encountered spoke English. To an extent, I managed to communicate with them speaking basic Spanish, and of course at the clinic the interpreter was always around.

I began this trip wanting to stay home and see to Alia's care, but fortunately it was easy to call to and from Central America, and I was encouraged to hear my daughter was progressing nicely. Only then could I thoroughly enjoy the good we were able to do performing cataract surgeries and restoring sight for dozens of grateful Panamanians.

19
Ethiopia

*Salt comes from the north,
gold from the south, and silver
from the country of the white men,
but the word of God and the treasure
of wisdom are only to be found in Timbuktu.*

WEST AFRICAN PROVERB

In 2003, the Rotary Club of Pittsburgh, Pennsylvania, planned to make a humanitarian visit to two Ethiopian cities. Although I am not a Rotarian, one of the club's ophthalmologists had backed out of the trip after preparations had been made for him. The club contacted SEE International, which, in turn, contacted me about the medical mission.

At that time, Ethiopia had only sixty-eight ophthalmologists in the entire country to serve its 70 million people, according to the Rotary Club briefing. Most of the doctors had trained at the local university, and few had the chance to go to other countries for additional training. Because of the scarcity of ophthalmologists, none would be available to provide postoperative care. Under these conditions, SEE would not normally sanction the trip. But the Rotary Club chairman requested special permission on my behalf since the alternative was to do nothing at all.

Our group of forty-seven consisted of retired lawyers and judges, doctors and their wives, nurses, and others from Pennsylvania, Illinois, Florida, and even England. Becky Klungersetter, a pleasant and highly competent perioperative nurse whom I worked with in Orange County, and I were the only volunteers from the West Coast. I had known Becky for a few years, and since she had always expressed an interest in going on a medical mission, I invited her along to help me evaluate patients for surgical care.

Along with two other ophthalmologists, the group included orthopedic surgeons and obstetricians/gynecologists as well. Becky and I flew to Pittsburgh to join the team. As we all assembled and made our introductions in the airport, I realized this was the largest group I had ever traveled with on a humanitarian mission.

The two other ophthalmologists on the trip were both excellent surgeons. Dr. Robert Shindler from Pennsylvania, who had retired, was also trained at Wills Eye Institute, five years before I was there doing my fellowship training. And Dr. David Moss of London, age seventy-five, performed surgeries faster than I could. He had gone on numerous medical missions. One evening in the Debre Berhan Hospital cafeteria as we talked over our dinner, Dr. Moss asked me where I was from originally. When I answered "Burma," he raised an eyebrow and shared a story with me.

Dr. Moss had been to Burma on a medical mission, accompanied by his wife. She found the country's poverty and lack of even the most basic resources, such as antibiotic eye drops, quite disturbing. Upon returning to England, she wrote an article in a local newspaper reporting these unacceptable conditions.

"The Burmese ambassador saw the article and forwarded it to Burmese officials. They notified us that she was barred from ever returning," Dr. Moss told me, shaking his head in disgust. He listened intently to how I was able to get out of Burma. And having witnessed the country's oppression and destitution, he understood my passion for undertaking medical missions to help the world's most desperate citizens.

Our trip to two central Ethiopian cities took me to Addis Ababa, the capital of Ethiopia, and to Debre Berhan, about five hours' drive north. During our eight days in Ethiopia, the three of us performed more than one hundred surgeries for patients with cataracts, pterygium, and various other conditions. Four transplantable corneas donated by the Eye Bank Orange County were also put to good use in patients with impaired vision due to trauma and infection.

This impoverished country was yet one more place where I saw more pathology in ten days than I would see in ten years in my home office. Regardless of the diagnoses, the people's vision problems rendered them unable to contribute to their families and required the time and resources of a sighted person to look after them.

Every time I travel, I bring candy, chewing gum, and granola bars. After examining young patients I give them a tasty treat. In Ethiopia, and subsequently in Haiti, I was amused that the children were rubbing their eyes to make them red so they could be seen as my patients.

We traveled everywhere in a large public bus that could accommodate our entourage. The hotel where we stayed in downtown Addis Ababa was unique in that many of the guests were adoptive parents. Most were Europeans and a few were Americans, and I observed at least ten couples with black infants. I asked a hotel worker about this phenomenon. He explained in a matter-of-fact fashion, "They usually stay here for about three months to bond with the infants. This is to ensure they can handle parenthood before signing adoption papers and leaving the country."

In Addis Ababa we visited a school for the blind. We brought medications in the hope that some of those students were sightless due to curable infections or inflammations, but we found no such cases. Almost all were so-called medically blind (unlike legally blind, where there is still some sight), meaning "no light perception." Their conditions were probably the result of complex causes. Outside the school sat a young man of eighteen or nineteen years of age who had walked from miles away upon hearing that eye doctors from America would be visiting. I examined him and found he was completely blind in both eyes, and unfortunately we could not help him as both eyes had atrophied. When this was explained to him through an interpreter, the high hopes he had built were crushed. With tears streaming down his face, he refused to return home. Before we left, one of our team members suggested to him that he take advantage of the school's instruction in Braille and training in daily living activities, but in his inconsolable, distraught state, I'm not sure he heard.

To accommodate our large group in Debre Berhan, we were lodged in an old trade school that had been temporarily closed for us. Some beds were brought in, though not enough for everyone, and I was content to sleep on the floor. In another area of the school where other volunteers were to sleep, a pipe burst and all the floors had to be mopped dry.

The school was located across from the hospital. Every day as I looked out the window, I would see a group of young children, some no more than five or six years of age, gathered outside. I'm always interested in children, so I went out and asked them through an interpreter what they were doing. "Going to school," was the polite reply.

"May I go with you?" I asked. The interpreter responded that the school was located at least three miles away and the children walked there. And most of them had no shoes. Now I understand why Ethiopians so often win marathons! And my entire time there I don't believe I ever saw an overweight person.

During our stay, a female lawyer from Chicago supervised what we ate. She made sure that even the salads were washed with clean water. But in spite of her diligent efforts, about fifteen members of our group became ill with dysentery, sore throats, and general malaise, including my roommate, Becky. After three days in bed, and with tea and sympathy from me, she was able to rejoin us.

Near the end of our time there, the Swedish ambassador in Addis Ababa, who was a Rotarian, treated us to an elegant dinner at the Sheraton Hotel. As soon as we left the hotel, we saw a line of beggars waiting outside, having heard that visiting Americans were inside.

One of the most difficult aspects of the trip for the others and me was adjusting to the Ethiopian timetable,[1] which is different from that in most of the world. I was prepared to work hard but was surprised when I was told that the hospital representative would pick me up at 2:00 in the morning. After the Ethiopian clock was explained to me, I realized the time was actually closer to 8:00 in the morning.

Because Ethiopia is located near the equator, the sun rises and sets at the same time throughout the year. At dawn as the sun rises in Ethiopia, Ethiopians start their clock and call that time 1:00 in the morning—about the same time of day we call 7:00 a.m. Ethiopian midday and midnight are 6:00.

At the end of our visit, we hired a tour guide, an Ethiopian student working on his doctorate at the local university. He was fine featured with bronze skin and neatly trimmed hair and spoke English fluently with a thick Ethiopian accent. As politely and gently as I could, I inquired about the Ethiopian way of keeping time. "Why," I asked this well-educated young man, "would your country not want to keep time the same way as the rest of the world? Why not make things easier by using the same timetable as we use in America?"

I was surprised when he asked, equally politely, "Is America mentioned in the Bible?" I responded that I hadn't read the Bible in such detail. With conviction and obvious pleasure, he replied, "America is never spoken of, but Ethiopia is mentioned forty times. And since the Bible states that the sunrise marks the beginning of a new day, so it is."

It was hard for me to argue with that.

20
Sri Lanka

Although the world is full of suffering, it is also full of the overcoming of it.

HELEN KELLER

A few months after the devastating tsunami hit Southeast Asia on December 26, 2004, I arrived in Sri Lanka to help. As one of the worst disasters in Sri Lankan history, the tsunami took the lives of tens of thousands of people and the homes of many more. I had been inquiring as to how I could contribute there and finally found out about what was called the Foundation of Goodness' Rainbow Clinic. This foundation supports an eye clinic eighty miles south of Colombo, the Seenigama Rainbow Clinic. The rainbow signifies the staff's willingness to care for any patient in whatever capacity they can.

SEE had not been to Sri Lanka before, and its emphasis is surgical eye expeditions and teaching in underserved communities, not responding to natural disasters. But given the aftermath of the tsunami, the tremendous need, and the headache I was giving SEE about the crisis, SEE honored my request and gave me supplies for emergency eye care.

Along with the surgical supplies, including a donated sterilizer, I brought about thirty implants. I doubted that I would be able to do any surgeries, not knowing the conditions I would find locally. Moreover, I didn't know any ophthalmologists there.

My daughter Sufia, a public health student at Johns Hopkins Bloomberg School of Public Health, accompanied me to Sri Lanka. Also along were a UCI medical student named Bishoy Said (he became a doctor in 2012) and Bishoy's friend from Saint Louis University in Missouri, Raymond Azab. Although I had not met Raymond before, I readily agreed to have him join us. With their help, we easily lugged a considerable amount of supplies.

After arriving and meeting our group in Colombo, we and our supplies were escorted to Seenigama. Along the way we saw nothing but destruction. It took four and a half hours to travel eighty miles, with roadblocks, fallen trees, and rubble everywhere. Broken seashells littered the streets and yards. We stayed in a small hotel, Coral Rock Hotel, one of the few places still inhabitable and intact.

The next day we went to the clinic and found out that doing any intraocular surgery would be unwise, if not impossible. The clinic had been hastily set up in a house that belonged to a wealthy sugar cane merchant from Colombo named Kushil Gunasekera. During the tsunami he was in that summer beach house with his children, but when the water started coming they were fortunate to escape. When the water receded, he went back and to his pleasant surprise saw that his well-built brick house was still there and hadn't been washed away. This generous gentleman quickly repaired the house and donated it to an organization that could use it as a clinic for the half-million people living within walking distance of the United Nations camp.

Doctors from Colombo were lending a hand at the clinic whenever possible. A female ophthalmologist in that town had her house and office washed out, so she couldn't help while I was there.

I also visited the 1,560-bed Karapatiya Teaching Hospital, but it had no room there for me to do elective surgeries. Because of the loss of the

450-bed Mahamodara Maternity Hospital, Karapatiya Hospital devoted as many beds as it could to delivery services. Karapatiya is the main teaching hospital and the only tertiary (advanced treatment) referral care center for the southern province of Sri Lanka.

With the help of two women who were local social workers, Rushmini and Radheka, I quickly set up a makeshift eye clinic on the porch since offices in the house were being used as a communications center to contact the rest of the world. Only a few extraocular, minor emergency/urgent ophthalmic procedures were done. When I had to have a patient lie down to remove a foreign object from his or her eye, we used the floor or a bench. I was glad we had with us devices to check for glaucoma and retinal problems. The drops we brought for infection, inflammation, and treatment of glaucoma were fully utilized. The implants and surgical supplies that were not used were left in the clinic for a local ophthalmologist to employ when the situation stabilized and the local hospital operating room could reopen for procedures.

During a break, one of the young women working in the clinic office took me to a place within walking distance of the clinic. With a heavy heart and tears in her eyes, she showed me her four-year-old son's burial place, which was along a walkway since the lack of space didn't allow for a separate ground for a cemetery.

A woman in her seventies whom I treated for a minor eye infection had no idea where her family was and no way of finding out their whereabouts. This woman's home was gone, and she found herself staying on a roadside, not even having a tent in the United Nations camp because she hadn't lined up and been assigned one. As I talked with her, she revealed that she was a devout Buddhist. She was consoled by her belief that if she suffers in this life, maybe her family would be spared from suffering. I found her hope in this ancient concept of yin-yang remarkable. Later I visited a temple where a large number of people were attending services, particularly women and children. Although these are not my beliefs, I respected their faith, especially in this time of disaster.

After a couple of days in Sri Lanka, a group of osteopathic medical students from Pomona, California, came to help us and provide much-needed relief for my team. Sufia, Bishoy, and Raymond had never witnessed such massive devastation before. I tend to become numb when tragedies threaten to overwhelm me, focusing instead on doing what I can to help. But with Bishoy in particular, I could clearly see his deep sadness in his downcast face, and I felt a day off would do them good.

I suggested that an Australian woman who I had been told was building a school just a few miles away from the clinic could use their energies in a number of capacities. The three of them went there and stayed all day helping carry construction supplies to the site.

That evening as I rode in a Jeep on my way to pick them up from the construction site, a large palm tree fell on the road a few hundred feet in front of us. The driver and I were thankful to not be crushed, but the tree kept us from driving farther. We got out and walked around it, picked up the students, and brought them to the Jeep to go back to the motel. The weather, structures, and environment in general were precariously unstable.

Still, I was glad I had suggested the outing for these students because the next day I could see their countenances had changed. There was more confidence and less depression on their faces. And the Australian woman was very pleased to have had three young, English-speaking volunteers from America give her a hand. The students and I left there glad about what we had accomplished but saddened by the overwhelming loss and suffering.

On our way back, Kushil invited us to his Colombo house, where he provided a nice meal and thanked us profusely for coming. His mother, almost eighty, also lived with him. She was waiting to see me since she heard an eye doctor was visiting. I listened to her regarding her eye health and checked her with my portable instruments. I reassured her she was okay, and she was delighted to have an American doctor examine her.

We heard that the hardest-hit area was north of Colombo, so I volunteered to go there for a day, assess the situation, and see if I could help someone else from SEE go there and staff a clinic there. However, I was strongly advised against it. I learned that Colombo had been waging a fierce campaign against the Liberation Tigers of Tamil Eelam.[1]

Time magazine later called the Tamil Tigers "one of the most organized, effective and brutal terrorist groups in the world" and stated, "Through their history, the Tigers have financed their operations with bank robberies and drug smuggling, among other illegal acts."[2] These militants were engaged in a decades-long civil war to become an independent state that has cost thousands of lives—military and civilian—on the island. Even during the tsunami crisis, rebel activity was prevalent and volatile.

It would be another five years before their leader was killed and the Sri Lankan military would defeat the Tigers. As a result, the situation improved tremendously and Kushil has been able to extend the Rainbow Clinic program into that area. A few years after my visit to Sri Lanka, Kushil came to the United States to raise funds for his Foundation of Goodness and the Learning & Empowerment Institute he had helped form for North Sri Lanka. This Institute's mission is to provide and foster essential community services including medical care; English and technology education, business skills and women's empowerment; children's development; environment management; moral and cultural development activities; a preschool, elders' home and orphanage; and sports development programs to engage the rural poor.

While in Southern California to fundraise for the project, Kushil came to see me for an eye exam and diagnostic testing. "You wanted to go to North Sri Lanka and it wasn't safe, but it is now," he assured me with a twinkle in his eye. He continues to strengthen Sri Lanka by uplifting and empowering his country's poor and disadvantaged.

21
India

*It is health that is real
wealth and not pieces
of gold and silver.*
MAHATMA GANDHI

In 2005, a representative from SEE International contacted me in response to a letter from Nysasdri Organization, an NPO/NGO in India whose mission is to empower the area's most vulnerable members of society. The organization requested that an ophthalmologist visit and a YAG laser be donated to Kalinga Eye Hospital & Research Centre (KEHRC), which was building a new facility to replace a smaller structure that it had outgrown.

The laser was needed to facilitate quick and safe capsulotomy, a procedure performed to eliminate the cloudiness that sometimes interferes with a patient's vision after cataract surgery. While SEE didn't have any lasers for that purpose at that time, its ongoing philosophy is to foster "dignity in the midst of poverty" however it can. I gave an emphatic yes and set about planning a January 2006 solo surgical expedition, from which I would report back on what I observed.

According to a 1990s estimate, more than one-third of the world's total blind population of 35 million live in India.[1] This is largely due to poverty and a lack of healthcare to eradicate cataracts. Located on the east coast of India, Orissa is among the country's poorest states, with more than 40 and as much as 65 percent of the largely rural population living below the poverty line.[2] KEHRC is the only eye hospital in central Orissa. It's a nonprofit facility that provides free eye-care services for the poor. The hospital had opened just four years earlier as a clinic in a small house and had expanded significantly to bring sight-restoring outreach to a primarily rural population.

After my sixteen-hour flight, an aide from KEHRC met me at Bhubaneswar Airport. Bhubaneswar is the capital of Orissa and a major Hindu pilgrimage center known for its more than five hundred Hindu temples.

The driver greeted me with a slight bow and, hands pressed together, said, "Namaste. Our founder and director, Mr. Sarangdhar Samal, welcomes you and thanks you for coming. We have made all the arrangements for your stay." We loaded my boxes of medicine, implants, and my minimal personal belongings into his car and were on our way, driving past shanties and people milling everywhere. Men rode on bicycles and motorbikes. Women in vibrantly colored saris corralled their children. People were packed into and on top of buses. Along with this sea of humanity, several times we had to stop for cows since they're considered sacred to India's millions of Hindus and freely roam the streets.

Following a two-hour drive, we arrived in Santhasara, the small village where I stayed and worked. As is customary, I gave the driver a handsome tip for his services. A hospital official had arranged for my lodging in a small guesthouse within walking distance of KEHRC. I was grateful that it had indoor plumbing and a full-time housekeeper. Some of the nurses and employees who lived too far to commute also stayed in this two-story structure. It was especially popular during the monsoon season, when the bus didn't run. After my arrival in the village the sun was setting, so I unpacked, showered, and turned in early to be ready for the next day.

While there were some distinct practice and cultural differences between United States hospitals and KEHRC, I found that the hospital was run with great efficiency. Upon my arrival, a nurse manager gave me a tour. She showed me the operating room and patient pre- and postop areas, where dozens of patients sat cross-legged on the floor. "Early in the morning, a hospital bus picked up patients who live in villages two hours or so from the hospital," she explained. "After arriving they were fed breakfast and evaluated for cataract surgery to be done later this morning and this afternoon; then they will be taken back home the following day."

Although I held my tongue, this routine of feeding patients a breakfast of *aaloo puri*, a round bread filled with spicy potatoes, struck me as odd. In the United States, providers are adamant about patients not eating anything after midnight or even having a drink of water in the morning preceding a cataract surgery. Back home, I've had cases cancelled when a patient violated this edict. But as I reflected on the process, I realized that these patients weren't receiving general anesthesia, which often causes nausea and vomiting, and if a patient's vomit is inhaled into the lungs it can lead to a serious infection or pneumonia.

The patients who had come from a distance stayed overnight, many sleeping in a shed behind the hospital. One of my cataract patients, emaciated and with weathered skin, looked quite old. When I politely asked her age, I discovered she was years younger than my sixty-two years. She told me she had no surviving relatives, yet she seemed to be in good spirits. "The reason I'm still alive is I must have done something good in my past life," she shared with quiet conviction. "My suffering here will lead to a better quality of life in my next life."

"Having cataract surgery should definitely improve your quality of life in your immediate future," I responded.

One morning I accompanied a technician on the minibus going to a small local village where patients were lined up for eye examinations.

The village had no clinic, so they used a room in the school to screen the patients before bringing them to the hospital. As a precaution to prevent infection, the patients were given antibiotics and underwent probing and irrigation of the nasolacrimal (tear) duct to prevent obstruction of tear drainage after surgery. This is not commonly done in the United States in conjunction with cataract surgery, but it was done here to prevent postsurgical, retrograde infections caused by dusty, dirty irritants in the environment.

At that time, the hospital did not have any ophthalmologists on site. Each week, a young ophthalmologist named Dr. Debabrata Sahani from a town several hours away traveled by bus with his wife and toddler daughter to work at KEHRC. This tall, slender doctor was very well trained and handled a remarkable volume of surgeries. Each afternoon he amazed me as he performed thirty to forty cases, literally tending to patients to his left, right, and center. I had never before seen anyone work so quickly and efficiently. He had six teams, each with three people, who worked in the preop, operating room, and postop areas. However, he confided that he was planning to leave, as the commute was taking its toll on him.

I helped with the surgeries but was very slow compared to this doctor. In one afternoon I could handle about five cases compared to his thirty or more. He used a technique common in India called manual small incision cataract surgery (MSICS). This technique yields comparable surgical outcomes to phacoemulsification, the technique of choice in developed countries. While both phacoemulsification and MSICS achieve excellent visual outcomes with low complication rates, MSICS is less expensive and requires less technology, although surgical recovery times tend to be much longer.

I believe that any surgeon worth his or her salt should have a passion for improving technique, no matter where it is found. I was so impressed with Dr. Sahani's surgical technique that after a week with him I decided to venture out and visit the place where he had been trained—Aravind

Eye Hospital. I called and let the hospital administrative staff know I wanted to visit, and they responded very positively, offering to show me around their facility.

After taking a taxi back to Bhubaneswar, a plane to Kolkata (also known as Calcutta), and a second plane to Madurai, I found a taxi to Aravind Eye Hospital, the largest volume eye care facility in the world.[3] Thirty ophthalmologists were employed there and performed more than six hundred cases a day. About 70 percent of the patients received free services, with the rest paying on a sliding fee scale.

I was welcomed by the administrator of Aravind, Dr. Aravind Srinivasan. He is the nephew of the late Dr. Govindappa Venkataswamy, founder of the Aravind Eye Hospitals and a venerated pioneer of mass eye care delivery. The youthful Dr. Srinivasan was professionally dressed in a suit and tie and carried a cell phone that was constantly ringing. He was well organized, giving me a printed schedule as to how I should spend my day touring the hospital. Aravind's administrator earned his MBA while specializing in finance at the University of Michigan. He had previously visited SEE International in Santa Barbara. When he asked where I was from and I told him Orange County, California, Dr. Srinivasan's eyes lit up. "I am familiar with this county. It's very affluent and it's where Disneyland is located," he remarked.

During my hospital visit, I was able to observe some eye surgeries, as this modern facility's operating rooms had cameras with monitors outside the OR for viewing the procedures. I met two ophthalmologists from the United States who had gone to Aravind for fellowship training in MSICS. I knew of one resident from UCI Medical Center's Department of Ophthalmology who had applied there but had not been accepted, most likely because of the large number of residents from throughout the United States applying to work at Aravind. A group of visiting Japanese ophthalmologists was there that day to learn how to design and operate an eye hospital on a large scale.

Diljo Thomas, a slightly built and highly motivated young man who was working on his MBA in hospital administration, walked me around the hospital campus and gave me a tour of Aravind's adjacent facilities. The Lions Aravind Institute of Community Ophthalmology is a training facility to educate health-related and managerial personnel in the development and implementation of efficient and sustainable eye-care programs in India, Asia, and Africa. Next door, at a manufacturing facility called Aurolab, intraocular lens implants used in cataract surgeries were produced. At that factory I spoke with a sales representative, who told me the implants were sold for one dollar and seventy-five cents each. They were also exported to eighty-nine countries throughout Asia and Africa for two dollars each. I was so shocked I made him repeat what he said. Those prices are a far cry from costs charged in the United States, which are four hundred times as high.

As we walked, Diljo told me about Aravind and peppered me with questions about hospitals and practicing in America. "Is it true that doctors in America are besieged with legal problems?" he asked.

"Yes," I admitted, "we have to be very careful and follow a lot of rules, but we have plenty of ophthalmologists, operating room staff, and resources, so we're not as hard pressed as doctors seem to be here. I've noticed that your doctors don't have any time to talk, but back home we're not mass producing thirty surgeries a day per doctor." I didn't tell him this, but for every one of my cases, I have to sign and date eleven documents, which definitely hampers my productivity.

At Aravind, the revenues from the one-third of its patients who can afford low-cost care are used to subsidize treatment for the two-thirds who cannot pay. A key factor in Aravind's ability to operate at a low cost is the absence of lawyers bringing lawsuits against providers. As we in America struggle to make healthcare affordable, perhaps we can learn some lessons from Aravind's highly efficient, community-building model of care.

At the end of the tour I thanked Diljo for such an interesting and enlightening tour. He smiled and responded, "I've learned more from you than you did from me."

In 2008, the Bill & Melinda Gates Foundation gave the Gates Award for Global Health and its $1 million prize to Aravind Eye Care System.[4] In 2010, Aravind received the world's largest humanitarian award, the Conrad N. Hilton Humanitarian Prize and its $1.5 million purse to advance Aravind's cause.[5] The awards were presented in recognition of the groundbreaking work done at Aravind to prevent debilitating blindness and provide affordable eye care to the poor. According to the Gates Foundation website, "Thanks in part to Aravind's efforts, the estimated number of blind people in India fell from 8.9 million in 1990 to 6.7 million in 2002, a decline of 25%."[6]

Both Aravind and Kalinga were vibrant examples of how sightless people who cannot help themselves can be empowered to not only enjoy seeing the world around them but also become more independent and productive members of society. After returning home I wrote an e-mail to SEE, confirming that indeed a large volume of eye surgeries was being performed in a quality manner at KEHRC, in spite of its limited resources. The gift of a YAG laser would certainly be well deserved for this growing, altruistic center for vision restoration.

I was very comfortable during my two weeks in India since the weather was pleasantly warm and I know three of the local languages. Yet it was heart wrenching to know that one hundred thousand indigent people in Bhubaneswar alone slept in the streets each night. I took comfort in knowing that for at least a few, we had removed their cataracts and with them a major obstacle to a better life.

India still has massive problems, but there are glimmers of hope. Along with its sight-saving initiatives, I was impressed to see many female doctors and professionals working alongside their male counterparts. As stated by the country's first prime minister, the late Jawaharlal Nehru,

"You can tell the condition of a nation by looking at the status of its women."

It was certainly a memorable visit to the land where I was born. Nine months after visiting India, the land of my ancestors, I would return to Myanmar, the land of my youth.

22
Myanmar (Burma)

*I've never tried to block out the
memories of the past, even though some
are painful...Everything you live through
helps to make you the person you are now.*

SOPHIA LOREN

In the summer of 2006, I was in my office seeing my patients when I received a phone call from a general surgeon in Hawaii, Carl Lum, MD. "I was given your name by SEE International," he relayed, "and I'm calling on behalf of an organization called Aloha Medical Mission based in Oahu, Hawaii. We plan to take a medical mission trip to Myanmar this October. We don't yet have an ophthalmologist going, and since you're originally from there, we'd like to have you join our team."

I immediately accepted Dr. Lum's invitation and started working on my office schedule, as well as the time I would have in Sagaing, a region in northwestern Myanmar. I am very familiar with this town, which is a holy place in Myanmar, just as Vatican City is in Rome. In Myanmar, the vast majority of the 50 million people are Buddhist, and Sagaing has more than five hundred monasteries and six thousand monks. I remembered from my youth that everywhere one looks there are men, women, and children with shaved heads wearing saffron yellow robes, far outnumbering laypersons.

131

The Aloha Medical Mission group tours one of the many ornate temples in Sagaing. *Photo courtesy of Aisha Simjee*

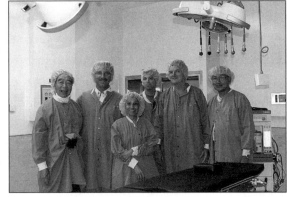

The Aloha Medical Mission group in the OR. *Photo courtesy of Aisha Simjee*

One day soon after Dr. Lum's call while I was working in the St. Joseph Hospital operating room, anesthesiologist Alain Wu, MD, a trusted colleague I worked with for many years before he retired, asked me if I had any other mission trips planned. He may have intended to only make polite conversation, but I responded with, "I'm going to Burma in October. It would be a big help having your skills in such a remote place. Why don't you come with me?"

To my pleasant surprise, he answered, "I'd like to go."

"I'm sure that can be arranged," I said, hoping he would follow through. Despite Dr. Wu's unfamiliarity with Myanmar, his never having been on a mission with Aloha, and the expenses such a trip would require, he was true to his word.

As our departure drew near, I stayed in touch with Dr. Lum to work out the trip logistics. He warned me, "Aisha, you must not identify yourself as an immigrant of Burma nor speak Burmese once we arrive. We don't want any problems." I knew that his caution was warranted, and the last thing that members of our party would want was to be detained in Myanmar. I readily agreed to heed his advice and sent him my passport. Without a hitch, he was able to obtain visas for me and sixteen others making the trip.

Finally, Dr. Wu and I were on our way to meet the other members of our team in the relatively small airport in Yangon. The others were from Hawaii. Dr. Lum introduced us to our fellow travelers; our welcoming host, who represented the area's *sayadaw*, meaning "chief monk"; interpreters; and a few extra helpers to assist with our large load of luggage. The host was a small, elderly man wearing the traditional long skirt called a *paso* worn by local males. He came up to me while I was standing at the customs office, looked me in the eye, and asked me in clear Burmese, "Aisha, do you remember me?"

Astonished, I searched his face but didn't recognize him after so many years. I wondered if I should acknowledge who I was or pretend I was a different person. When I shook my head, he went on to say, "My shop was located next to your father's shop. Don't you remember how you used to run over to play with my daughter, and I would give you a treat?" He gave me his exact address in Yangon and added, "I heard a few years ago that you had left the country after graduating from medical school."

At that point I realized who he was and started speaking to him in Burmese. If I hadn't, I suspected that my facial expression would have given me away anyway. As soon as I could, I politely excused myself to find Dr. Lum. I quietly informed him that U Han, who had volunteered to greet and receive guests from foreign organizations and help get us on the local flight to Mandalay, was an old family acquaintance. Dr. Lum looked around, protectively placed his arm around my shoulder and assured me in his kind and dignified manner, "There's no use worrying about it, Aisha, I'm sure we'll be fine."

We flew to Mandalay, the royal capital of Myanmar, and then took an hour-and-a-half bus ride to Sagaing. U Han sat down by me, and we began talking like old friends. He asked me for details about my family, and I asked him about his daughters. "They have all left the country for different parts of the Western world," he replied, a hint of sadness in his voice. "I live alone in downtown Yangon. I miss them, but I'm honored to dedicate my time as a volunteer for Sitagu Sayadaw."

Just as Myanmar's ruling military regime refused help after the devastating 2004 tsunami, it also didn't want medical missionaries to provide humanitarian aid. Thankfully, the venerable Sitagu Sayadaw welcomed our visit. Around 1980, Sayadaw Ashin Nyanissara founded the Sitagu International Buddhist Missionary Association (SIBMA), which is devoted to alleviating the suffering of all people. One of the welfare projects of SIBMA is Sitagu Ayudana Hospital. This being under the sayadaw's domain, located in a temple, the local government did not interfere, and as a result, everything went smoothly.

We worked and stayed at Sitagu Ayudana Hospital, located in Sagaing Hills, Myanmar. The sayadaw converted part of the massive temple into a hospital in order to serve people regardless of caste, race, and economic status. The hospital depends on charity to sustain its work.

Dr. Carl Lum converses
with a young Burmese
monk. A vascular
surgeon from Hawaii
and medical director of
Aloha Medical Mission,
Dr. Lum also served
as team leader for my
2006 trip to Burma.
Photo by Aisha Simjee

Upon our arrival, we were taken to the ornate, whitewashed stone temple and greeted with open arms by the sayadaw and his entourage of male monks and female assistants called sisters. We were welcomed with comfortable beds, water, and bouquets of flowers. The sayadaw's appearance, with his shaved head and a robe covering one shoulder, reflected his cultural and religious heritage, but he also holds two doctorates—from schools in Australia and Austin, Texas. Thus, he was able to speak to us in English, albeit with a heavy accent. But when I spoke to him in Burmese to thank him for his hospitality, he clasped his hands and beamed with delight.

As I often do, I brought my portable surgical instruments, but soon discovered most of them wouldn't be needed. The hospital had an operating microscope, a working sterilizer, and adequate supplies to perform general surgery. I was also pleased to find it had dependable electricity with a backup generator, since there is a severe power shortage in Myanmar and electricity is available for only a few hours daily.

We began working the next day. Since I had no language problem, the interpreters spent all their time with the other volunteers—a pediatric surgeon, an obstetrician/gynecologist, an internist, and nurses, all from Hawaii except Dr. Wu and me. Because we were now under the Sayadaw's protection, I could freely speak Burmese.

I screened patients and selected them for surgery. Many of them presented with red, tearing eyes, and rarely did they have any financial resources. A good number of the patients were local monks and sisters. They were very humble, soft-spoken, and enormously grateful. Each day I performed cataract extractions and repairs of ectropion, a painful turning out of the eyelid; entropion, a turning in of the eyelid; and pterygium, a noncancerous growth of the clear, thin tissue (conjunctiva) that lies over the white part of the eye (sclera). A few hours per day were reserved to evaluate and treat nonsurgical patients for various eye diseases. Patients young and old came from as far as the northern cities of Meiktila, Myitkyina (located near the border of China), and Mogok, the gem city of Myanmar famous for its rubies and sapphires.

Although conditions have improved in recent decades, Myanmar still has one of the world's higher prevalence rates for the infectious disease trachoma, as well as leprosy, tuberculosis, and malaria. I saw several stages of trachoma in patients. Several of those patients had painful lid pathology and visual impairment caused by the disease. I recalled having trachoma as a child and was chilled to think that I could have been in their predicament.

Dr. Wu was there to administer anesthesia for my patients and the other specialists' patients and to help screen surgical candidates. That made my work efficient and productive, and we were able to do about thirty-five cases in all.

My ability to speak the language was appreciated by my Aloha colleagues. On an outing to go shopping in downtown Mandalay, a couple of hours' drive by bus, my fellow workers all wanted me to bargain for them. The shopkeepers in the open market and small boutiques thought I was a local person there to help a tourist group. "Too much!" I would tell them firmly, and invariably they would agree to a lower price.

The group was especially grateful when I helped out in the kitchen, explaining to them what each dish was that we were eating. One of the sayadaw's sisters cooked our meals on a huge black coal-burning stove. She prepared a variety of Burmese dishes, most of which were different kinds of fish cooked with coconut and various Burmese spices. Everyone felt comfortable eating the food and in fact enjoyed it. After my absence of thirty-six years, I relished the preparation of breakfast dishes called shwethamin, kaung-hnin-mok, and paybyoke, all made with different kinds of rice and grains.

One afternoon after I finished my work, I walked by myself to another temple farther up the hill and was rewarded with a fantastic view of this region, known as the Land of Pagodas. One morning I woke up very early and took a walk to a local school for young children who were all being trained to become monks. In their culture, it is customary for any family with more than four or five children to send one to the monastery to become a monk. I saw highly disciplined children, who every day would wake up with the sunrise, say their prayers, and eat a light breakfast, consisting mainly of a thick rice, jaggery (similar to brown sugar), and coconut. They were very polite when I greeted and chatted with them. "Are you studying hard?" I asked, and they responded solemnly, "Yes *sayama*," which means teacher.

On our last day there, the sayadaw organized a social gathering and prepared a feast for all the guests. There were local performances of music and dancing. The Hawaiian group sang their Hawaiian state song, and all of us danced a slow, smooth, hand-gesturing Burmese dance to traditional music.

Fortunately, after years of keeping the country shut to outside people, officials had finally realized they should open it to tourism. As a result, after our work in the hospital we had an opportunity to visit the palace in Mandalay and temples in Pagan. We even visited a temple with twelve hundred steps up a hill. I encouraged most of my colleagues to make it to the top and we did, resting every couple hundred steps.

When we flew back to Yangon, I said goodbye to Dr. Wu, Dr. Lum, and the rest of the group. I am grateful to Dr. Lum. Through Aloha Medical Mission he has provided a great deal of help to Myanmar, although the country has not made it easy. Myanmar refused foreign humanitarian aid when Cyclone Nargis devastated its delta region in 2008. Aloha Medical Mission was the only organization allowed to assist, but only because the sayadaw was its sponsor. The Aloha team boarded a floating clinic and treated patients up and down the Irrawaddy River.

Now well into his eighties, Dr. Lum recently told me his wife asked him when he would retire. His response was inspired by the words of English theologian John Wesley:

> Do all the good you can,
> By all the means you can,
> In all the ways you can,
> In all the places you can,
> At all the times you can,
> To all the people you can,
> As long as ever you can.

Since I was in my homeland, I wanted to spend three days visiting with relatives and looking for old friends. Daw Tin Hla is married to my cousin U Thun Lwin, and they invited me to stay in their home. Their daughter, Tin Tin, was the last child I had sponsored and welcomed into my home in California. Tin Tin bears a strong resemblance to her mother of Chinese heritage, both with pretty, almond-shaped eyes and sallow skin. Whenever I've introduced Tin Tin as my daughter, I've seen the puzzled look on people's faces.

Daw Tin Hla came to the airport to pick me up. When we found each other, she hugged me and began to cry. "I never thought I'd see you again," she managed to say.

She graciously took me to visit some of my other cousins and tried to help me track down my old friends. As it turned out, many of them had died or left the country, but I did find two of my closest friends from elementary school. Retracing my steps taken decades earlier, I knocked on these friends' doors and when they opened I smiled, said hello, and asked, "Do you remember me?" They did, probably because I haven't changed much. There had been no way to contact them about my visit, and they were shocked to see me. I found both women living in the same houses as they were in almost four decades ago when I'd left the country. By this time we were all in our early sixties, and they were great-grandmothers. Word got out that I was in town, and a friend from as far away as Prome, 180 miles to the north, called to ask me to come and see her, but unfortunately time didn't permit me to go.

I visited my old schools, including my medical school and the hospitals where I trained. Returning to my old neighborhood in downtown Yangon, I felt deflated as I surveyed a rundown urban inner city. The grand downtown of a booming port city that once took pride in its stately colonial buildings from the early 1900s and immaculate landscaping was now but a shadow of its former self. Once commanding but now dilapidated, blackened structures and overgrown foliage served as stark evidence of the neglect and careless management by the ruling junta in recent decades.

I had looked forward to visiting the house where I grew up, a four-story domicile built at the behest of my parents. In my family's care it had always been impeccably clean, but it, too, had fallen into an unkempt state of disrepair. I walked up the broken cement steps and surveyed the cracked and peeling paint on the outer walls, originally beige and now a dirty brown.

I knocked on the door and was greeted by a middle-aged Burmese man and his wife. I explained that I had once lived there and asked them if I could come inside. They ushered me in, delighted when I offered them a small gift of hard candies from America. The prominent crystal chandelier that I remembered was gone, and undergarments hung in front of the windows. *Mother would be grieved to see her home*, I thought. Young student nurses from Yangon General Hospital were renting rooms in the house and came and went during my short visit. The couple offered me green tea and asked me to stay for a meal. I politely declined but thanked them and went on my way.

Knowing that I would be visiting my cousin, my old neighbor U Han came by and tried to persuade me to go with him to Pyaymyo (formerly Prome) and see my ancestors' house and the ancient temple that my great-grandfather contributed money to renovate. Being an eye doctor, I found it interesting that a temple in this small town houses the famous "Buddha with spectacles"—considered to be the only one of its kind in the world. But because of time limitations, I just couldn't go.

In the reunions I did have, all the people asked me to take their children home with me. Their appeals tore at my heart, but I had to tell them no. If I were a mother living there, I would have asked, too. And as often happens after I return home, an interpreter kept sending me e-mails, asking me to send him money and help him come to the United States. The oppression in Myanmar that has led to such desperation is a national tragedy. While I sympathize with the people's plight and feel sad that I can't do more, I'm simply not able to grant such requests.

When my husband picked me up at the airport, he gently asked, "Why so solemn? I would expect you to be happy to have gone back to Burma and come home again, but you seem a little depressed. Are you tired?"

"I'm pleased with what I accomplished on my mission, but I'm sad that I saw little if any progress in the past thirty-six years," I admitted. It was such a bittersweet reminder of my past. Still, the experience made me all the more grateful for where I am today.

In 2007, the year after my visit, the ruling junta unexpectedly raised fuel prices, prompting tens of thousands of Burmese to march in protest, led by prodemocracy activists and Buddhist monks. The government brutally suppressed the protests, killing at least thirteen people and arresting thousands more. Since then, the regime has continued its raids on homes and monasteries to arrest persons suspected of participating in the prodemocracy protests.

Opposition leader Aung San Suu Kyi, released from house arrest in 2010, appealed to all those who wish Myanmar well to help by "criticizing us when necessary, encouraging us at the right time and, if I may request it, providing us with practical help when we need it."[1]

In 2011, Senator John McCain traveled to Myanmar.[2] At the conclusion of his trip he wisely stated, "Government that shuns evolutionary reform now will eventually face revolutionary changes later."

Later that year, Secretary of State Hillary Rodham Clinton visited Myanmar. Her trip was symbolic of renewed yet cautious optimism concerning reforms. In covering her overture, Reuters reported, "There are no skyscrapers in Yangon. No gleaming shopping malls. Certainly no subway system. Its rutted sidewalks are laced with treacherous holes and broken slabs of concrete. Myanmar's former capital and biggest city is a crumbling monument to almost half a century of isolation and mismanagement at the hands of generals who took power in a 1962 coup . . . Today, chronic power outages and deteriorating buildings are constant reminders of decades of troubles."[3]

My Burmese friends and I have been very encouraged by recent events suggesting political change. I recently heard from Dr. Lum, who verified the improvements, commenting, "Hawaii has many Burmese-American physicians. For our first mission in 2006, not a single one joined us for they feared that when they returned to Burma, their passport would be confiscated and they would not be able to return to Hawaii. For our next mission, five of them will join us."

I can only hope that going forward the leaders of my native land will embrace progress and continue down the road to democracy.

23
Egypt

There are two ways to live:
you can live as if nothing is a miracle;
you can live as if everything is a miracle.
ALBERT EINSTEIN

Several times, including in 2004, I was invited to give lectures on the UCI campus to the medical student association regarding selecting a specialty for university students continuing into medical school. During my hour-long talk, one of the students asked me what I saw as the advantages of choosing ophthalmology as a specialty. "I'd have to say that what I like best is that it's adaptable to medical missions," I responded. "With limited resources and without the need for a highly sophisticated operating room, you can restore vision and completely change patients' outlooks and prospects for a better life."

Among the students who heard me speak was Bishoy Said, an Egyptian-born second-year medical student. He had grown up in Visalia, California, with his internist father and pharmacist mother. After the lecture, this handsome young man with curly black hair and dimples approached me and shared that he had a particular interest in going on medical missions. "I'd like to join you on your next trip. Do you think that would be possible?" he asked.

"Yes, I can always use help," I answered. A few months later, as it turned out, Bishoy accompanied me to Sri Lanka (see chapter 20).

In 2006, Bishoy discovered that St. Mark Hospital in Alexandria, Egypt, had a large backlog of patients needing eye surgery but had limited resources. He had visited the hospital, attached to the massive St. Mark's Cathedral, with his Coptic Christian family. His father, Onsy Said, MD, had been there to offer his medical services on several occasions.

The Coptic Church has a worldwide following, but its roots and headquarters are in Egypt. While Islam is the official state religion and nearly 90 percent of the population is Sunni Muslim, an estimated 8 to 12 million Egyptians are Christians, primarily Coptic Christians around Alexandria, Egypt.[1] I had visited Alexandria years before as a teenager with my family. When Bishoy called to invite me to join his family on a medical mission to St. Mark's, I was immediately taken with the idea and began making arrangements.

Before departing, Bishoy observed me doing cataract surgery at St. Joseph Hospital and spent time in my office on Saturday mornings to observe me performing eye examinations. He learned about all the basic equipment we would be using. Bishoy could barely contain his excitement about our upcoming trip.

SEE had agreed to send supplies with me for fifty cataract surgeries. I, on the other hand, had agreed to bring along an aspiring medical student. I told internist Kusum Ohri, MD, a colleague at St. Joseph Hospital, about our trip and she asked, "Would you consider having my twenty-two-year-old son, Anuj, accompany you? Anuj will soon be graduating with his bachelor's degree and he's considering a career in medicine."

"I would be delighted to have his assistance," I told her.

Anuj and I reached Cairo a day after Bishoy and his parents did. We brought an ophthalmoscope, a hand-held slit lamp for eye exams, and an Alcon surgical microscope, which the customs official would not allow me to take to Alexandria. Bishoy's father, Dr. Said, went to high-level customs officials in Cairo, but they would not budge. They wanted the microscope inspected by the health department, and it was against the rules to bring such a big piece of equipment into the country. The best they could do was promise it would be returned to me when I left.

After wasting an entire day, with a disgusted sigh Dr. Said announced, "I think it's best to leave without the microscope and move on to Alexandria."

We piled into a rental car, headed north, and about two and a half hours later arrived in Alexandria. It was a ten-minute drive from the hospital to the elegant hotel where we stayed, a beach resort overlooking the sparkling waters of the Mediterranean. The Saids generously insisted on picking up the tab, which I had been planning to pay.

Soon after arriving, Anuj and I drove to the hospital in the bustling downtown. We were pleased to see that the hospital's operating room was well organized and fairly well equipped, with a functioning ophthalmic microscope. A hospital official had notified the church congregation of our arrival and we had no lack of patients.

Dr. Susan Ramzi, a middle-aged Egyptian ophthalmologist with neatly combed black hair and kind black eyes, began helping me screen surgical candidates. As we worked, we discussed various ophthalmic diagnoses that she had seen in the local clinic. Because of a lack of resources, she rarely performed surgery. I was impressed with how dedicated she was, working full time in the hospital's eye clinic and the church's convalescent home. As we worked side by side I happened to mention, "While I was volunteering in Abeokuta, Nigeria, I mistakenly diagnosed osteogenesis imperfecta [a serious condition associated with deafness and brittle bones] because of a malfunctioning microscope that cast a blue light. Patients appeared to have blue sclera [white of the eyes], which often comes with this condition."

She turned to me and exclaimed, "I helped in Abeokuta, too! What are the odds that a doctor from America and a doctor from Egypt would both work in the same Nigerian clinic?" The shared experience helped us to bond quickly, and we planned our surgical days together from the next day onward. For eight days I performed manual small-incision cataract surgery. Dr. Ramzi went on to provide the patients with postop care.

I shared information with the local ophthalmologists about the efficacy of phacoemulsification, which at that time they had no access to at St. Mark Hospital. They became enthusiastic about the phaco because of its extremely low complication rate and quick recoveries. The hospital CEO contacted a German manufacturer of phaco machines with an office in Cairo, and a woman I took care of was wealthy enough to donate most of the $40,000 toward its purchase.

On my last day there, Dr. Ramzi arranged for me to make rounds with her at the convalescent home. I enjoyed talking with patients through an interpreter. Since we were there on a Sunday, some of the patients' families were on hand as well. I soon realized that the residents didn't need my help with their eyes, but they were delighted that a female doctor all the way from California was there to evaluate them. They really just wanted to talk. I felt like I was as much a social worker as I was a visiting ophthalmologist.

After returning to Cairo, Anuj and I took the opportunity to see one of the seven wonders of the ancient world, the Pyramids of Giza, and go to the local museum. I was particularly interested in showing Anuj an exhibit I remembered from my first visit to Egypt when I was just a few years younger than he: hieroglyphics of eye surgery recorded on papyrus by the Egyptian scribes some two thousand years ago.

According to local lore, around the same time, Jesus Christ performed cataract surgery for blind people around Jerusalem. Although accounts of Jesus healing the blind in the gospel of Mark don't verify this claim, could it be, as was suggested, that in some cases he would touch the eyeball, apply a little pressure, and dislocate a hypermature cataract into the vitreous (gel portion of the inside of the eyeball) to restore sight?

Bishoy and Anuj told me how much they enjoyed their time in Egypt. Bishoy was very patient in teaching Anuj how to use the slit lamp and ophthalmoscope, and Anuj was a fast learner. By the trip's end, Bishoy confided, "I've made up my mind to become an ophthalmologist." Anuj announced, "This trip has helped me decide to become a doctor. I'm definitely going to medical school." Anuj has two brothers who are both computer engineers, and I was glad that his mother's hope for one of her children to choose a career in medicine could be realized. At the time of this writing, Anuj was in medical school and planning to specialize in ophthalmology.

In early 2011, my heart sank as I read reports on the Internet and in the newspaper about the Egyptian revolution and violence in the region. In January at least seventeen people were killed in a car explosion in front of St. Mark's Cathedral.[2] Many more were killed in the "Arab Spring" that followed.

While I doubt I will return to Egypt anytime soon, I will continue to mentor young medical students, some of whom I hope will take up the cause of sight restoration. In April 2011, I again had the opportunity to share with UCI medical students. This time, it was in the context of a Medical Student Speed Mentoring event held at UCI. Along with several colleagues in other medical specialties seated in a classroom, I spent just four minutes answering each student's questions about my profession before a bell would ring and the students would switch seats. The event was thoroughly enjoyable and beneficial for tomorrow's doctors, and I look forward to participating again in the future.

24
Colombia

*Some men see things as they are
and say, why? I dream of things
that never were and say, why not?*

ROBERT F. KENNEDY

S udeep Kukreja, MD, serves as a neonatal-perinatal medicine specialist
on staff with me at St. Joseph Hospital and adjacent CHOC Children's
Hospital. He is also someone who asks, "Why not?" and is the founder of the
NPO/NGO organization Arpan Global Charities (AGC). In 2007, an Arpan
team led by Dr. Kukreja went to help the indigenous people of Colombia.

Arpan is a Hindi word meaning "dedication" or "to give." Focused on
service and education, Arpan provides free medical services to medically
underserved populations of the world, and health education to local medical
students through volunteer medical trips to these underserved areas.

I was asked by St. Joseph Hospital colleague and obstetrician/
gynecologist Allan Akerman, MD, and office manager, Paula Tobon,
to join the group as they traveled to a village near Bogotá. I, in turn,
invited UCI medical student Bishoy Said, who had accompanied me
to Sri Lanka in 2004 and Egypt earlier that year. Along with them, Usa
Aroonlap, another medical student at UCI, was also pleased to join the
trip to further her understanding of pediatric psychiatry. She was eager
to learn what she could about the children of the Arhuaco Indians.

Also making the trip were a neurosurgeon from St. Joseph Hospital's medical staff, Hector Ho, MD, and his son, along with physicians and nurses from Cedars-Sinai Medical Center in Los Angeles and other Southern California hospitals. I was pleased that I would accompany this group and that an anesthesiologist I work with, Manoj Kulkarni, MD, would also go and help with anesthesiology services, which would make my work much easier and faster.

I had more than a traveler's share of luggage with an ultrasound machine (to measure the implants), an autoclave (sterilizer), a portable laser, and a supply of fifty cataract lenses. I also brought a slit lamp worth about $8,500 that was generously donated by ophthalmologist Sara Jones-Gomberg, MD, from Kaiser Foundation Hospital in Panorama City, California, as a gift to the local Colombian hospital. It had already cost $350 just to professionally package this delicate, three-foot-by-three-foot device, so I was glad when my colleagues volunteered to share the luggage weight so I would not have to pay extra for the overage.

We touched down in Colombia's capital, Bogotá, a city of more than 7 million people. From there we flew to Valledupar, close to the Caribbean Sea on the northern tip of South America. For many years the city had been heavily affected by Colombian infighting and had been rife with kidnappings. We knew it was dangerous for a group of American doctors, who would be tempting to those looking for ransom prospects. Fortunately, police were guarding the local roads we traveled. I believe we had Paula to thank for alerting officials and ensuring our protection, along with her influential Colombian family.

Hospital Rosario Pumarejo de Lopez in Valledupar is a multispecialty hospital with a well-equipped operating room and competent nursing and OR staff. Once we were settled, I started screening patients and with Dr. Kulkarni's help selected surgical candidates.

It was a blessing to have such capable assistance, and we were able to perform cataract surgeries efficiently on a number of patients. I shared the surgical schedule with the other medical personnel. Dr. Ho performed an intricate ventricular peritoneal shunting to relieve increased pressure inside a patient's skull due to excess cerebrospinal fluid on the brain, as well as lumbar laminectomies to alleviate pain in patients with degenerative spinal conditions.

Here is Dr. Kukreja and his team's account of our visit, recorded on Arpan's website:

> Twenty-three volunteers from California made up the team including nurses, echocardiogram technician, occupational therapist, medical students, gynecologists, pediatricians, neonatologists, a neurosurgeon, an ophthalmologist and a few non-medical volunteers. The main activities were held at Rosario Pomarejo Hospital in Valledupar, where more than 600 patients, mainly from the local indigenous group called the Arhuacos, were seen and treated. 163 procedures such as eye surgery, gynecological surgery, neurosurgery and echocardiograms were performed. In addition, the pediatricians and neonatologists treated several hundred patients at outpatient clinics in three different remote villages in the region and at two other clinics in the city of Valledupar. These were patients belonging to the local indigenous groups—the Arhuacos and Kankuamas. There was a tremendous amount of cultural and educational exchanges throughout the mission, between the visiting team and the many native Colombian medical and non-medical volunteers. The team got to experience the lush greenery and the beautiful mountainous countryside of the region's villages at Crespo, Jwerwa and Nabusimake.
>
> At the end of the mission, the Arhuacos held a ceremony to give thanks and gave each member a small

token of appreciation. Thanks to the hard work and support of the Fundación EsCultura and its members, AGC was able to accomplish its goal of working with the local indigenous people. This was another great educational and service experience for the team.[1]

For me, the best part of this trip was having an operating room and support staff available every day into the late hours to accommodate the backlog of surgeries there. On the first day in surgery, I worked with a local OR nurse until 11:00 p.m. She became ill and couldn't help the next day. Instead, I worked with a cardiovascular surgical nurse, Shelly, from Cedars-Sinai Medical Center until midnight. On the third day, I worked with Bishoy and Usa until 1:00 a.m. to catch up with a heavy surgical load. On the following days, Bishoy and Usa took turns assisting me in the OR well past midnight.

Many children and some adults I observed had kwashiorkor and a few presented with marasmus, both caused by malnutrition. I shared these findings with the pediatricians and nurses of CHOC Children's Hospital. While they may have read about these conditions, kwashiorkor and marasmus are rarely seen in the United States. *Kwashiorkor* is actually an African term that can be translated as "the first child when the second child is born." In some cultures, this is the time the first child is no longer breast-fed and is likely to suffer malnutrition.

As much as I enjoyed aiding the people, I was also discouraged by dishonesty. Even my white lab coat embossed with my name and logos from St. Joseph Hospital and Magnet (the hospital's designation for nursing excellence), left overnight in the hospital staff locker room, was gone in the morning. A local ophthalmologist took implants and other supplies I was giving to the hospital. And, while I intended to provide free surgeries for Colombia's most needy, I discovered that some of the patients I operated on were from the local doctor's personal practice. It angered me that he was profiting from my efforts, but I kept my suspicions to myself. I would be leaving and needed his help following up on the postop patients.

Once back in Bogotá, I took advantage of my time and visited Clinica Barraquer. The late José Barraquer, MD, considered the father of refractive surgery, hailed from a family with four generations of prominent ophthalmologists. Originally from Spain, in the 1950s he moved to Bogotá where he founded the Barraquer Institute of America, training many of the ophthalmic surgeons practicing around the world today. Barraquer furthered the improvement of suture material and technique in cataract and corneal surgery and designed numerous surgical instruments, including some that still carry his name. His life's work, however, involved the reshaping of the cornea to change the eye's refractive power, which laid the groundwork for LASIK and other modern lamellar procedures. All three of Dr. Barraquer's children became ophthalmologists, including one in Colombia and one in Barcelona. His daughter practices ophthalmology in Texas. I was pleased I had a chance to visit this renowned institution, still very popular in South America.

Coincidentally, in 1995 I visited Barraquer Eye Centre in Barcelona, Spain, which is one of the oldest eye hospitals in southern Europe. I was there to visit my daughter Sufia, who at age fourteen was a student at Phillips Academy in Massachusetts and spending a year in Barcelona. She had always been adventurous, and I felt that if she were to go abroad, Spain would be a good choice as she could learn Spanish, an important language for a Californian in public service.

As for my service in Colombia, I have fond memories of what was accomplished, having labored with such highly competent and motivated humanitarians.

I look forward to a mission trip to Ecuador with my Arpan colleagues in the coming year.

25
Cambodia

Wherever you go,
go with all your heart.
CONFUCIUS

In January 2010, just weeks before I had planned to embark on a medical mission to Cambodia, a massive earthquake rocked Haiti. I wanted to go to the stricken nation immediately, but I had already committed to visiting Cambodia in February. I anticipated my trip to Southeast Asia would be worthwhile, and I wasn't disappointed. My skills were put to good use, performing restorative procedures for sight-deprived patients with cataracts and eye diseases, and teaching local doctors new techniques.

Our humble patients brought their own bamboo mats for a place to sleep and wait patiently for their turn to be examined. In Cambodia, about one in three people live in poverty.[1] The nation struggles with a shortage of medical personnel, training programs, infrastructure, and facilities.

According to an article in *Ophthalmic Epidemiology*, the prevalence of blindness and low vision in Cambodia is relatively high in comparison to other developing countries, yet the majority of the causes of blindness and low vision are treatable or preventable. Cataracts account for about

Patients and families wait outside the Lions SightFirst Eye Care Center in Phnom Penh. *Photo by Aisha Simjee*

two-thirds of Cambodians' blindness.[2] Land mines, explosions, and other war-related events have also been a significant cause of ocular injury in and around Phnom Penh, Cambodia.

The receiving organization for my trip was Chey Chum Neas Hospital in Phnom Penh. Much of its financial support comes from a partnership with the Lions SightFirst program. Having witnessed how well the Lions' vision centers in Panama and Kenya functioned, I anticipated that this hospital would be fairly well equipped and well managed, and it was.

The hospital officials recommended that I stay just a few miles from the facility at the Goldiana Hotel. Its multistory facade is inspired by traditional, temple-style Cambodian architecture. Virtually all the hotel's guests came from different parts of the world as volunteers for humanitarian causes. Each morning the guests would gather for the complimentary breakfasts and share what brought us to this corner of

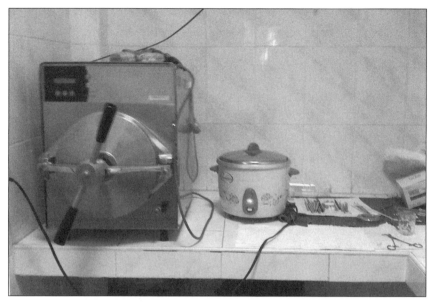

A rice cooker takes the place of an inoperable equipment sterilizer—a common sight in developing countries' operating rooms, such as in this Cambodian OR. *Photo by Aisha Simjee*

the world. I had the chance to meet several of them: an English teacher for young children, a pediatrician, a family practitioner, nurses, a social worker, and faith-based missionaries. I also met the hotel proprietor, a woman who appeared to be in her midforties and who inspected the complimentary buffet breakfast early each morning. Knowing I was a visiting ophthalmologist from America, she approached me about her husband, who was blind. It was easy to engage in conversation with her since, like most people, she knew someone with eye challenges and wanted to hear my opinion. "My husband is legally, irreversibly blind," she told me in English and introduced me to him, an elderly gentlemen holding on to a white cane. Although he had already been examined by specialists and they knew he would remain sightless, I commiserated with her.

Phnom Penh is the capital and largest city in a country of about 14 million people, yet its healthcare services are underdeveloped. Most of

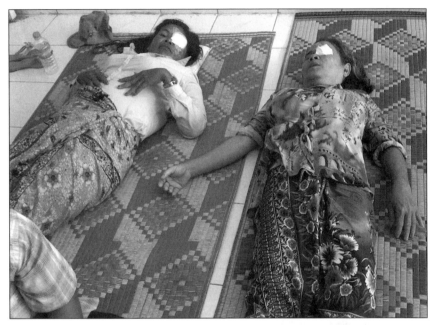

The recovery room in the Eye Care Center in Phnom Penh. *Photo by Aisha Simjee*

the local people who can afford to travel visit Singapore or Malaysia for their medical and surgical services. However, the local doctors were capably performing cataract surgery.

I hand-carried two corneas with me, closely guarding my precious cargo halfway around the world. The first cornea was used in a private clinic operating room of a prominent local ophthalmologist to make use of the cornea at the earliest possible opportunity. The second keratoplasty (cornea transplant) took place at the hospital. I also packed amniotic membrane required for pterygium surgery, and residents from neighboring provinces came to observe the procedure.

My intention was to leave behind the medicine and frozen tissue that I brought for eye care at Chey Chum Neas Hospital, but it had no refrigerator to keep these perishable items. I asked one of the local ophthalmologists to escort me to a nearby appliance store, bought a

Neuroophthalmologist Dr. Kenn Freedman and I with residents at Chey Chum Neas Hospital in Cambodia. *Photo courtesy of Aisha Simjee*

standard-size refrigerator, and had it delivered to the preop area of the hospital. The next day, I opened the refrigerator to find it filled with the staff members' lunches! I chuckled and had the interpreter tell the staff, "It's fine to utilize the refrigerator for personal use, as long as you leave one shelf for the medical supplies."

Some of the locals seemed surprised when they met me. I suppose I didn't look like the person they were expecting. For the most part, Cambodians (like people in many developing countries) who hear an American doctor is coming expect to meet a tall white man, not anticipating the diversity we have in America. There was, in fact, a tall neuroophthalmologist from Texas Tech in Lubbock named Kenn Freedman, MD, PhD, stationed at the hospital to teach residents.

While in Phnom Penh, I visited Preah Ang Duong Hospital, the local university hospital where Dr. Freedman taught. His medical subspecialty, focused on the relationship of the eye with the central nervous system, rarely brings him to an operating room. He welcomed my visit to share surgical expertise with the physicians in training. There I met residents in different levels of training. I was pleased to see that several of them were women. In Cambodia, as in many developing countries, women tend to suffer from discrimination, yet their empowerment will be essential for the country's modernization. I found these young women to be just as enthusiastic as I had been when I was in training, and I became all the more optimistic about the country's ophthalmic progress and future.

During my time in Cambodia, I had a chance to glimpse its ancient history. In the town of Siem Reap, 192 miles from Phnom Penh, the enormous temple, Angkor Wat, is considered in some circles to be one of the seven man-made wonders of the world. It even appears on Cambodia's national flag. Built in the twelfth century, it is a fascinating temple surrounded by a moat, crowned by five spires, and displaying mysterious stone faces and other carvings from ancient Hindu mythology. As awesome as this architectural wonder is, it was another, more recent historic landmark that I found beyond comprehension in its devastating impact.

Esther, the wife of the hospital's chief of staff, an Australian Cambodian, took me to the "S-21" (Security Prison 21) Tuol Sleng Genocide Museum in downtown Phnom Penh. Formerly a high school, this disturbing facility was used by the Khmer Rouge communist regime to imprison and interrogate an estimated fifteen thousand people during the late 1970s.[3] We also visited Choeung Ek, about fifteen kilometers south of Phnom Penh.[4] When there was no more room to bury bodies around the S-21 prison grounds, this became a mass grave site. I shuddered at the horrific sight of massive clear acrylic cases filled with thousands of victims' skulls from pits where bodies have been exhumed from these killing fields. An estimated 1.7 million people, or about 25 percent of the country's population at that time, were cruelly executed or died of disease and starvation following the Vietnam War.[5]

The Khmer Rouge regime was toppled in 1979 but only after it had committed one of the century's worst crimes against humanity. Decades later, the nation is still struggling to heal from the ravages of its civil war.

Although I wanted other medically skilled volunteers to travel to Cambodia with me, no one I knew would commit to the mission trip. Repeatedly, medical students and nurses express interest in going and ask me if someone will pay their way. My response is always the same: "Sending and receiving organizations rarely have the money to fund these expeditions; it's up to you and me to finance our own travel." Everyone I've known to make this small investment has never regretted his or her decision.

26
Haiti

Cure sometimes,
treat often, comfort always.
HIPPOCRATES

Haiti's catastrophic magnitude 7.0 earthquake hit on January 12, 2010. I watched and listened along with the rest of the world as the news from Port-au-Prince flashed across the Internet, televisions, radios, and newspapers, showing traumatized Haitians who survived the disaster only to be entombed in rubble and chaos.

Immediately, people from around the world sprang into action. Military troops, firefighters, search-and-rescue teams, engineers, physicians, and healthcare teams boarded planes headed for Haiti. Humanitarian aid and pledges poured in, and prayers were said for the nation. James J. James, MD, DrPH, MHA, director of the Center for Public Health Preparedness and Disaster Response for the American Medical Association, urged well-meaning clinicians to use restraint. "The spontaneous volunteer has no place in disaster response," he asserted. "Volunteers must be part of the solution, not the problem. Don't go unless you are as [sic] part of an organized team or have assurance when you arrive that you will be joining one."[1]

The following days, as I continued to see patients in my office and perform surgery, Haiti's plight was never far from my mind. I contacted

SHINE Humanity's headquarters in Irvine to see how I could be of help and when it would be best to go. Meanwhile, within the next twelve days, fifty-two aftershocks rattled Haiti. Within a month, the horrific death toll was estimated to be 230,000 people.[2]

Knowing that the devastation would not recede with the news coverage, I set in motion plans to go to Haiti in the coming months and still maintained my plans to visit Cambodia in February. With the help of Comprehensive Disaster Response Services (CDRS), I arranged to travel to Haiti in April to offer my services in the massive relief effort, and I informed my family of my plans.

My husband questioned me, his brow furrowed in concern. "Have you done your homework? Were you able to establish good contacts in Haiti?"

"I'll be safe," I assured Sabi, insisting, "People are in need, and for some of them I might make the difference. I must go."

Understanding how strongly I feel about easing suffering wherever I can, Sabi has never tried to stop me from taking mercy mission trips. Instead, as he has often done, he told me, "Do what you feel is best. Only promise me, Aisha, that you won't bring home any children. I know what a soft spot you have for kids." In his own way, so does he. Although he doesn't have the same calling as I do, in his free time he's volunteered his talents as a treasurer for a local school and Boys & Girls Club of America.

Because SHINE was such a new organization, I contacted SEE and let people there know that I would be making the trip. They helped prepare my way by getting in touch with California congresswoman Lois Capps, letting her know of my plans. It wasn't long before the congresswoman had written the ambassador at the Haiti embassy asking him to help me if I ran into any trouble.

Three months later I said my goodbyes and boarded a plane to Haiti. I had planned to fly into Port-au-Prince, yet when I arrived, most incoming planes were being diverted. The runway was covered with

Flanking me are members of the US Army's 82nd Airborne Division, offering to do whatever heavy lifting was needed. *Photo courtesy of Aisha Simjee*

mud and water and was in no condition for planes to land safely. I had been told that if landing in Haiti wasn't possible, the plane would fly to the Dominican Republic. From there, passengers should plan on an eight-hour trek by bus. A colleague I met once I arrived had taken that long bus ride. Her pilot didn't want to take a chance trying to land in Port-au-Prince. I was relieved when our plane's wheels touched down, in spite of the precarious conditions. Looking out the window in the bright morning sun, I surveyed the bulldozed dirt and rubble flanking the airport's single runway.

Mansoor Khadir from SHINE met me at the airport. He was a well-built, middle-aged gentleman who was once a Venezuelan, then a Chicagoan, and ultimately a humanitarian in Haiti. Mansoor's driving talents were put to good use shuttling workers to relief campsites.

My first look at Haiti from the ground stopped my breath. It had been about ninety days since the quake hit, yet each direction I turned it

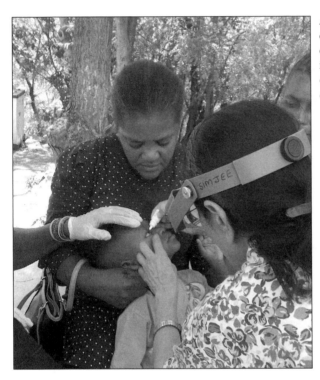

Administering eye drops in the infected eye of a child living in a Haiti earthquake camp. *Photo courtesy of Aisha Simjee*

looked like a war zone. Buildings had crumbled, leaving piles of concrete and mounds of rock standing several feet high. Trees had been shaken to the ground, now slowly dying. Many of the roads had chunks of asphalt lifted or missing, making them unusable. Alternate routes were now a way of life.

As Mansoor drove, I couldn't help but notice the people along the roads. "Where do they live?" I asked.

"Right here," he replied, making a semicircle with his upturned left hand. "Many of them are living right where you see them sitting. The lucky ones live in tents, under tarps, or in makeshift shelters made up of blankets or garbage sacks. Some have even found shelter in the wreckage of their former homes—living in the half that's still standing, however unsafe it is."

As he drove, I noticed the markings on the buildings and homes that were left standing. "What do the colors mean?" I asked.

"Over a hundred civil engineers have come from the US and Canada," he explained. "Their job is to go street to street, inspecting each structure and then grading them. A red mark means the risk is too high, and no one must enter the building. Yellow indicates that it is okay to retrieve belongings, but get in and get out quick. It's not safe to sleep in a yellow building. And the green means it's safe to move back in."

Without Mansoor saying so, I came to the conclusion that green was rare and that the majority of the buildings or homes were marked red—not safe for human occupation. No wonder people were everywhere, walking in 100-degree heat, carrying what appeared to be their only belongings in the world. I kept my concerns to myself, but wondered, *This devastation is worse than what I saw in Sri Lanka after the tsunami. Haiti was plagued with widespread poverty, bribery, and corruption before the quake. How and when will the people recover from this?*

Around noon we finally arrived at the Jenkins/Penn Haitian Relief Organization (J/P HRO) tent city, set up by philanthropist Diana Jenkins and actor Sean Penn.[3] As we parked, Mansoor told me that this site had been a prestigious country club in an affluent suburb of Port-au-Prince. "See there?" he said while pointing to a landscape peppered by eleven thousand tarp-covered structures. "Just three months ago that was a nine-hole golf course and tennis club. Today it houses about 55,000 displaced people. The large tent over there sits on what used to be tennis courts. That's the medical clinic where you'll be working."

I was welcomed to the camp by Alison Thompson, the medical coordinator for J/P HRO. The Australian-turned-New-Yorker, whose blonde hair hung in a long ponytail from under a baseball cap, made sure I had the supplies and assistance I would need. I later learned that as a preacher's daughter, Alison had visited third-world countries while growing up and cut her teeth as a humanitarian in her own right in the aftermath of 9/11, when she ran a first-aid station at Ground Zero for the better part of a year. She met Mr. Penn through her 2004 documentary *The Third Wave*, a film about her yearlong volunteer experience in Sri Lanka following the tsunami.

Alison saw to it that I was assigned a one-person tent, number thirteen, furnished with a thin foam mat and sleeping bag and situated a few steps from the tents of the other medical team members. I was introduced to nurses and paramedics from New York, Boston, San Francisco, and parts of Canada. I met several soldiers from the United States Army's 82nd Airborne Division who offered to do whatever heavy lifting was needed.

I almost never sweat. In the operating theater back home I've been known to throw a blanket over my shoulders to quell my shivers and stave off the chill that doesn't seem to faze my surgical team. But here, in the sweltering heat and humidity, I found myself wiping perspiration from my face and felt my shirt sticking to my back.

I went in search of water to clean up and then set about unpacking my supplies of antibiotics, steroids, and eye drops for ocular allergies and glaucoma. Before long, two Haitian women came and introduced themselves as Vanessa and Marjorie and offered their services as interpreters. They immediately pitched in to help me set up a treatment area and throughout my visits stayed by my side, translating French to English. They earned eight dollars per day and were grateful to be healthy and have jobs.

Others I met and would work alongside included Yusuf Harper, MD, an emergency physician from New York; Tiffany Fonte-Ordonez, MD, an internist from Colorado; Noreen Mirza, MD, a rheumatology fellow from Cedars-Sinai Medical Center in Los Angeles; and Colin James, RN, an educator for the San Francisco Paramedic Association.

Being a physician in Haiti was completely different from being in Orange County. My job morphed from ophthalmologist to emergency physician, plastic surgeon, obstetrician, and orthopedic specialist. As always, I listened to the patients' problems and sympathized as best I could. But the multitudes of people, the extent of their maladies, and their sheer desperation overwhelmed me. The Haitians had lost their health, homes, friends, families, and jobs. Many had lost hope of ever recovering their former way of life.

Right away I became a popular physician to see. I wanted to think it was because of my skills and abilities, yet I tend to believe it was because of the large boxes of granola bars and dried fruit I brought with me. The children had heard that I had food, so in single-file fashion they lined up to be examined.

We worked from sunup to sundown. Although the camp was chaotic and tension rose during medical emergencies, we relied on each other for support. Working side by side with a group of people we had never known before and at times not even knowing each other's names, we put the principles of practicing medicine to work.

Most days I saw thirty-five to forty patients. Along with treating patients with a variety of eye infections caused by foreign bodies, I also addressed cases of scabies, gangrene, malnutrition, and fractures. One patient, a girl about ten years of age with a disfigured, extremely swollen leg, was literally dragged in by two women. "Dr. Aisha," the girl's mother pleaded through the interpreter, "you must cut off her leg. My daughter is in pain and we can't continue to drag her around!"

As I examined the girl's engorged leg and thigh-sized ankle, I suspected filariasis, a parasitic infection transmitted through the bite of an infected mosquito. As much as I wanted to, I was unable to diagnose the condition accurately without the luxury of a diagnostic facility or laboratory personnel. I also knew that if it was filariasis, such swelling was a classic sign of late-stage disease. All that I could do was to provide her a crutch so that at least for a while she could walk on her own, but I silently grieved when I could not offer her a cure.

I did perform an amputation of a young girl's infected broken finger, and I removed a decayed foreign body and cleaned out a gangrene infection on the right side of a young woman's swollen face. Although I had to cut through her risorius muscle, which would prevent her from smiling, she told me she would be "smiling in her heart" because the pain would be gone.

During my training in Burma, I had delivered dozens of babies, and those skills enabled me to deliver two Haitian babies—a girl and a boy. A hardworking young Canadian nurse named Brandon helped me deliver them. In the tent culture where victims and rescue workers bond quickly, the doctor who delivers the baby names the child. As we tended to the laboring mother, Brandon grinned and asked me, somewhat sheepishly, "If it's a boy, can we name him Brandon?"

"I suppose," I answered, more concerned about my laboring patient. Once the baby boy arrived, we laughed and cooed, "Hello, Brandon." The tired and happy mother, who like virtually all the locals spoke French, had a hard time pronouncing the name. When her attempts continued to sound like "Braandoon," the child's namesake teased, "If you don't learn to say it correctly, you won't get the baby." We all laughed, and Brandon went on to teach the new mother how to care for her baby boy.

One day a young man arrived at the clinic with a very sick two-year-old boy. Presumably the father, he carried the child's limp body through the tent doors and placed him on the examining table. Right away I began to examine him. Dr. Tiffany joined me and came to the same conclusion I had made minutes earlier. The child's breath was shallow and his skin was an unhealthy gray and burning. He had a multitude of problems. His only chance of survival was if we rushed him to the hospital in Port-au-Prince. We summoned the driver of a pickup truck, and with the boy's father sitting up front, Dr. Tiffany and I piled in the back, sitting on two spare tires and holding our critically ill patient. Although the hospital was just five miles away, it took us an

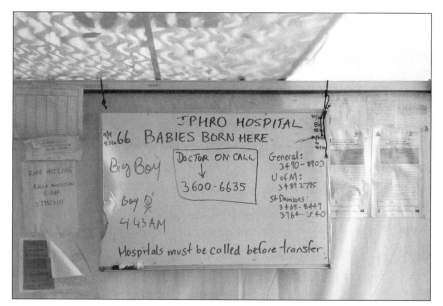

A news board for the volunteers in the Jenkins/Penn Haitian Relief Organization (J/P HRO) tent city. *Photo by Aisha Simjee*

hour and a half to navigate the damaged roadways. We arrived at the medical compound to find a makeshift tent hospital since the hospital itself had been red tagged, too unstable to be safe for patients and staff. We hurried inside the large tent to find help.

"I'm sorry," the nurse said through a translator, shaking her head while looking at the toddler. "We're not prepared to care for him."

I stood my ground and gently insisted, "But this child must be seen by a pediatrician without delay." Seeing we were determined and desperate, the nurse helped us clear a space on the floor where we could lay the child to await treatment. With the pale, crying child's father helplessly watching over him, Dr. Tiffany and I slipped away to be driven back to the Jenkins/Penn "country club." Dr. Tiffany expressed her doubts that the child would survive, and as much as I hated to admit it, I had to agree.

While I didn't know of Sean Penn or his body of work, I was impressed by how diligently he worked to help the Haitians. Each morning, I'd get up early to get in line for the restrooms. And each morning, Sean was already up and about with his colleagues, planning the day's activities. Not only had he come to Haiti to help, he had also brought along his son and daughter, both in their teens, and had put them to work. Sean had become an example to the world of how to help in times of need and a larger-than-life example to two teenagers who now knew it was possible to make a difference.

Early on I had met a fifteen-year-old mother. She had delivered a baby girl three weeks earlier. She slept in the camp and, with no place else to be, spent her days languishing just outside the camp's entrance. Since I'm usually a vegetarian who doesn't require much to eat, and with food at the camp being sparse, I began to bring her meat and other parts of the meals that were provided for me. Giving her food, I reasoned, would help ensure her breast milk wouldn't dry up. I told myself that I was feeding two people.

On my last day in Haiti the teen mother and her baby came to see me. Cradling her newborn, she began to speak with Vanessa, who relayed her plea: "Dr. Aisha, won't you please take my baby with you?"

Looking at her and then to the interpreter, I responded, "Do you know where I'm from?"

The young mother shook her head no.

I asked, "Do you even know where I would take her?"

Again she shook her head. Extending her arms and holding her firstborn child toward me as if I was going to take the baby, she began to sob. "You have given me food so that my baby will live. I know wherever you take her, my baby will survive." Telling her it wasn't possible to bring her with me and there was nothing more I could do broke my heart, but my husband's words not to bring home any children rang in my ears.

Before we parted, I took a picture of her and her baby, thinking that if I ever return I could look for her.

As I finished packing, Alison stopped by to thank me for coming. I left my remaining stock of granola bars and fruit snacks with her to use as she saw fit. "I hope we get the chance to work together again. Hopefully, it won't be in such a sad situation but a better one," she said, her smile tinged with sadness.

Saying goodbye to this nation that would take years to heal was difficult. After an intensely busy ten days, I felt I had barely scratched the surface in meeting the immense needs apparent at every turn. I boarded the plane in my slippers as the two pairs of shoes I had brought with me had "disappeared." When people are so desperate and have so little, they will take anything that might help them survive. The people in Haiti were crying for medical attention, shelter, food, emotional support, and even shoes. I took comfort in having witnessed international recovery efforts that were making a difference for hundreds of thousands of hurting people.

As I heard the roar of the engine preparing for takeoff, various situations from the past few days played like a movie through my mind. I thought of a toddler boy who clung to my leg long after I finished treating his sick baby sister, enamored with me for having given him one of the granola bars. I couldn't help but wonder, *What would my family say if they had actually witnessed this little boy hanging from my leg, as if I were his best hope for survival? When they saw his cherub's face and emaciated body, would they still insist on my not bringing home any children?*

Physically and mentally exhausted, I lay my head back on my seat. Before falling asleep, I prayed for the people of Haiti, appealing for healing in their bodies and homeland and asking that the world would not forget their plight.

27
Pakistan

We all have enough strength
to endure the misfortunes of others.
FRANÇOIS DE LA ROCHEFOUCAULD

A few months after the cataclysmic earthquake in Haiti, in July 2010 more than 14 million people in Pakistan were affected by the worst flooding in one hundred years.[1] Survivors urgently needed food, water, shelter, and medical care. International lenders estimated that direct damage to property and crops would exceed $9 billion.[2] United Nations secretary-general Ban Ki-moon stated, "The world has never seen such a disaster. It's much beyond anybody's imagination."[3]

I felt compelled to lend a hand and wanted to go immediately. But I had to wait for the arrangements to be made. Working with the sending organization, SHINE Humanity, and its field partner and receiving organization in Pakistan, Comprehensive Disaster Response Services (CDRS), I made a personal visit and plea to the Consulate General of Pakistan in Los Angeles to approve my visa.

Despite several letters written to the consulate by Laila Karamally, chief executive for SHINE, the date I planned to leave came and went and still I had no visa. Four days after my expected date of departure, I went to the Pakistan consulate in Los Angeles and politely asked the

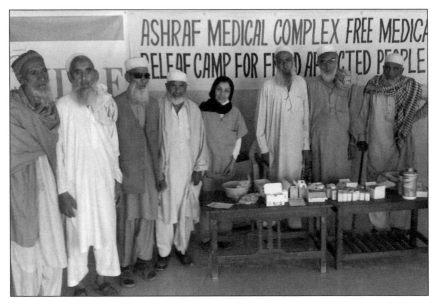

Standing with patients at a flood relief camp in Pakistan. *Photo courtesy of Aisha Simjee*

assistant consul to return my passport if the consulate was not going to give me a visa. I asked him, "Why are you holding up my paperwork? I am just a little eye doctor, but I'm experienced in medical missions and disaster relief work, and I'm ready to give a hand to those who badly need help. I've spent three hundred and twenty dollars on hepatitis A, typhoid, polio, and other vaccinations, and even more costly and wasteful, I made arrangements in my office to be gone right now!"

"It's not my decision," he replied with a shrug. "For a person applying with your background, I receive my instructions from Islamabad and they haven't approved it yet. But I'll see what I can do." I waited while he left the room, and about twenty minutes later he returned and gave back my passport and my visa. As soon as I had my documents in hand, I called the airport to book my flight. I finally

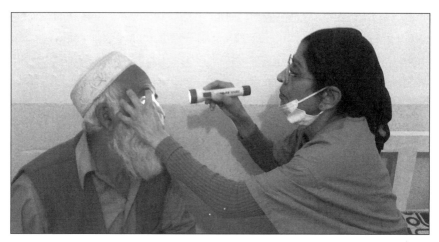

Examining a resident of a flood relief camp in Pakistan. I had to overcome cultural differences, as the men were not used to having a female doctor touch them. *Photo courtesy of Aisha Simjee*

reached Pakistan the first week of November, three and a half months after the flood calamity.

SHINE Humanity was registered as a public benefit corporation in 2009 and maintains an office in Irvine, California.[4] In January 2010, SHINE initiated its first international deployment to earthquake-stricken Haiti. Around that time I met the founder of SHINE and founder and executive director of CDRS, Todd Shea.

Todd was previously a musician by trade. He was organizing a large concert to be performed at the famed CBGB (Country, Blue Grass, and Blues) Gallery in New York City on September 12, 2001. Then came the 9/11 disaster. His concert was cancelled, and instead, he spent the next week working at the World Trade Center site, where he discovered his gift of coordination during disastrous, chaotic situations. As a result, Todd has completely changed his life. While once a cocaine addict, today he is drug free and a rescue worker to the world. When the 2004 tsunami hit Southeast Asia, Todd turned his shock and sadness into assistance, working in orphanages, helping build houses, and volunteering at a medical center. After the 2005 Pakistani earthquake, he arrived to help there and has stayed, starting an NPO/NGO. Todd has managed to make several trips to US cities to receive donations, mostly from Pakistani businessmen and physicians. He was in Pakistan when disaster struck again with ravaging floods, and has stayed to help people who would otherwise be without adequate healthcare services.

I flew to Pakistan with supplies provided by SEE International and personal purchase, which included ophthalmic anesthetic for urgent and emergent ophthalmic care, antibiotics and steroid drugs, syringes, natural tears, and other medical supplies. A CDRS representative picked me up at the airport. We drove about two and a half hours to Charsadda in the Khyber-Pakhtunkhwa Province, and I was briefed on how I would spend my time there, working in the flood victim camps.

I did not think it was possible, but the extreme flood devastation I found was even worse than what I had seen in Haiti. And, while Haiti has received some of the funds pledged for its plight, Pakistan has received relatively little assistance from the outside world. The waters have been slow to recede, and the packed camps for the displaced would be their home through the winter. They were subsisting on rations of rice and, if they were lucky, received blankets to warm themselves. Even the goats that they kept for their daily milk looked malnourished.

The few possessions the people had left were encased in mud. The dried mud caused cars and even bicycles to throw up clouds of dust. Children were covered in dirt—it was unavoidable. Women who had nowhere to wash their clothes or themselves were caked with mud. Everywhere I went smelled damp and musty.

The aftermath of the monsoon rains in Pakistan had manifested in skin diseases; upper airway infections; malnutrition, made worse with poor access to clean water; abdominal pain and diarrhea; and respiratory tract infections. When I was in Pakistan, in the fall the weather was turning cold, making conditions even more miserable and exacerbating the risk of disease for the thousands of flood camp victims.

Recovery efforts in Pakistan have included the building of some shelters for those lucky enough to acquire one. These homes, costing $600 and made to accommodate up to ten people, are made of cow dung and mud and last about two years. One corner is used for cooking and another as the restroom. They aren't much, but are certainly better than the camps, where most of the displaced Pakistanis found themselves. There was no electricity, only kerosene lamps and candles. The people slept on *khatlas*, which are cots with four wooden pillars and rope made from coconut running across them. In spite of the tents and camps erected, all the villages I visited still had people sleeping on the roadside.

I went to seven camps, all within a two-hour drive of each other. Since I didn't have much equipment or a clean facility for surgical interventions, the ophthalmology care I could provide was limited. With the help of two women, Uzma and Bilqees, both social workers, I set up makeshift clinics, borrowing a khatla where we put the supplies and a few chairs for the patients. Word spread quickly of my arrival, and hundreds of camp patients lined up to be seen.

About 50 percent of my time was spent in the capacity of an ophthalmologist, and the other 50 percent as a psychologist/social worker. Being able to speak the local language of Urdu made communication much easier, and I listened with a heavy heart to the people's stories of homesickness, the loss of loved ones, and concerns that the floods had washed away their children's future.

Dozens of patients were given bottles of eye drops appropriate for their conditions, including artificial tears to keep the eyes clean and moisturized and free of inflammation and infection. One of the recipients was a 118-year-old man with blurry vision and red, irritated eyes. I also saw a woman whose entire body was affected by leishmaniasis, the parasitic disease spread by the bite of the sand fly. A six-year-old boy whom I saw had been kicked in his eye by a horse. He'd had a ruptured globe, and a local doctor removed his eye. When he came to me, the orbital socket was infected with profuse suppurative fluid, or pus. I gave him antibiotic drops, eyewash, and sterile cotton pads.

Although I saw some injuries and diseases such as diabetic retinopathy that I could do little about, most of the patients I saw had eye infections. Those were bound to happen, given the poor hygienic conditions. I instructed the children not to rub their eyes and to wash their hands whenever possible.

Originally, a pediatrician, family practitioner, and nurse practitioner all wanted to come on this trip with me, but they all dropped out. One became pregnant, another became engaged to be married, and the third must have had his own reasons for not following through. My own family had expressed their doubts—I saw it on their faces and heard their concern. "Are you sure you can't find someone who can go with you?" my husband asked, thinking there was safety in numbers. But I had made up my mind and was optimistic I would make it back safely.

Because there are some inherent risks for an American citizen and physician traveling to the Middle East, a few times I've posed as a pediatric nurse from a health organization. Fortunately, I encountered no interference with my mission, but I would have posed as anyone to make the trip, except an exhibitionist. It's best to blend in, wearing local clothing and not attracting unnecessary attention. I will not let fear deter me, nor will I succumb to the hatred that motivates acts of terrorism.

Coincidentally, while I was there, Osama bin Laden was hiding in the same province, just fifty miles from where I visited, and his courier lived where I was staying, in Charsadda. Had I known, that would not have made a difference in my plans to go and help fellow human beings struggling to survive horrific conditions. Displaced and hurting men, women, and children, the elderly, and disabled people are not our enemies.

28
Peru

*It's not what you gather,
but what you scatter that tells
what kind of life you have lived.*

HELEN WALTON

Mission work takes more than a desire to travel to distant and exotic lands. It requires a strong commitment and sacrifice by anyone volunteering aid. In the weeks following my return from Huancavelica, Peru, I reflected on my time there and the logistical and physical challenges I faced to provide much-needed medical care. I have no regrets about going, in spite of some extremely harsh working conditions.

An estimated 52 percent of Peru's people live in poverty,[1] and Huancavelica is one of the poorest areas of Peru as well as South America. Its location high in the Andes Mountains isolates the community from health services. In fact, some of the Peruvians who live here never leave their mountain homes, subsisting on mining and farming atop the 12,800-foot mountain for their entire lives. Their life expectancy is a mere 56.8 years.[2]

The people of Huancavelica are primarily descendants of the Inca Indians, and most still speak the Inca language of Quechua. The Incan Empire was conquered by the Spanish who came in search of gold and silver, and many of the people are understandably suspicious of outsiders because of their history of exploitation. Their natural and chosen isolation has enabled them to minimize Western influence and preserve much of their distinct and ancient culture.

My attention first turned to Huancavelica when Steve Mora, MD, a young orthopedic surgeon on my hospital's medical staff, wrote in the hospital's physician newsletter about his trip there in 2010 and invited colleagues to join him for a two-week mission trip in 2011. When I contacted Dr. Mora, he was delighted to put me in touch with trip coordinator Ralph Kuon, MD, a Peruvian American vascular surgeon practicing in Whittier, California.

In 2011, Dr. Kuon was recognized by the California State Assembly for his tireless efforts to provide much-needed free medical services to the underprivileged in Peru. He has made several successful mission trips to Huancavelica through a joint effort of the Peruvian American Medical Society (PAMS), the Ministry of Health of Peru, the Buenaventura Mining Company Inc., and several charitable organizations. He has twice served as PAMS's president.

Speaking English with a heavy yet soft Spanish accent, Dr. Kuon shared with me the details of the mission. "It won't be easy to do elective procedures," he warned me. "You will encounter many obstacles when treating patients, including sparse resources, a language barrier, and limited medical equipment. You need to be aware that there is no heater in the hospital operating room or the clinic where you will be working. Be prepared for subzero temperatures since it will be winter when we arrive there in August."

Cold is especially difficult for me as a slight person. Back in California in the outpatient surgery center, I often wear a blanket around my shoulders until I step into the operating room. The operating rooms are kept cool for the comfort of most staff and because the lasers and other machinery tend to work best in a little below a normal room temperature.

Although I shuddered at Dr. Kuon's words, I braced myself and told him, "I've made up my mind that I would like to join you. I will be prepared."

I made a trip to the local sporting goods store, where I stocked up on thermal underwear and wool pressure socks. I began taking iron supplements, which would help me adjust to the high altitude. Along with warm clothing, I planned to bring antibiotics and other medical supplies and equipment such as my portable ophthalmoscope and slit lamp. I contacted SEE International, and its officials agreed to contribute supplies for ophthalmic assessments and treatments. I also took some surgical supplies for emergent and urgent surgeries, as was within the guidelines provided by SEE.

Many questions remained about the conditions I would find, leaving me feeling somewhat anxious. Would I be able to quickly adjust to the altitude? Would a nurse be available to assist with procedures? Would I even be able to perform surgery? After all, I would be following SEE's protocol, which would not allow me to perform surgery unless an ophthalmologist would be there to monitor the patients postsurgically. Therefore, I did not plan to do elective surgeries.

Apparently, the closest ophthalmologist was in Lima and came to Huancavelica only once every two to three months, working for four to five days. But would he or she be there during or after my stay?

Arriving at the airport for our departure, I was relieved to meet three local premed and psychology students who could help me carry my extra luggage. Dr. Kuon had given a talk to students at UCI, and several of them had responded to his invitation to join the trip. More than just receiving class credit, young, aspiring physicians taking a mission trip to a developing country gain invaluable perspective and I know the experience enhances their applications to medical schools.

For this trip, there was a mixture of local premed, medical, predental, and dental students, along with Dr. Mora, Dr. Kuon, and me. I was the second oldest volunteer after Dr. Kuon, a kindly looking gentleman with

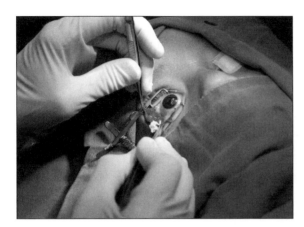

An orbital tumor is removed. *Photo by Mike Larremore*

receding silver hair. Every student was Asian except for one twenty-six-year-old male student and aspiring orthopedic surgeon, Michael Nieto. This tall, handsome young man with light brown hair would prove to be very popular with the children in the Huancavelica orphanage, where he helped pass out toothbrushes and taught healthy hygiene. The children were fascinated by their iconic American friend, and they all wanted his attention. Also on hand were Joan Weiss, MD, a pediatrician from Colorado, and her adult son, Mike Larremore, a photographer from Colorado.

Our group flew to Lima, Peru, where a plastic surgeon, an anesthesiologist, nurses, more medical students, and a social worker joined us. From there, we climbed aboard the full-size white bus, complete with a working restroom, that we found waiting for us. We set out on a twelve-and-a-half-hour trek on a long, winding road at top speeds of about thirty miles per hour. In retrospect, the trip there was easier than the trip back down, which took more than fifteen hours due to a massive rock falling onto the road and rendering it a one-lane thoroughfare. One of the members of our group missed his flight because of the delay and had to purchase additional airfare from another airline for nearly $2,000, since the airline he was on offered only one flight per week back to Southern California.

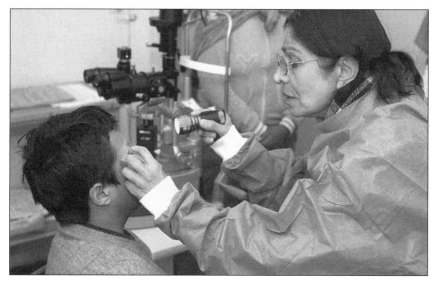

Examining a young Peruvian. *Photo by Mike Larremore*

Halfway up these majestic mountains, we stopped at a small but clean adobe-style hotel to become acclimated—and because the bus could not travel the road at night. One woman had become ill, probably with motion sickness, so she and another volunteer stayed behind until she was well enough to travel again.

Around midday on a Saturday, we arrived in Huancavelica and proceeded to the colonial-style Hotel Presidente in the center of town. The hotel was so close to the base of the mountain, it seemed as if I could open a window and touch it. At check-in when I voiced my concerns over the nighttime temperature plummeting to four degrees, the hotel staff gave me a small space heater to plug in beside my bed. It was a welcome companion as I wearily lay down to rest from the strenuous journey but not enough to keep me warm. I gathered every blanket and pillow I could find and piled them all on top of me while I slept.

The next morning, Dr. Kuon and some local people provided us with a briefing on the 120-bed hospital and orphanage housing about fifty children, along with our assigned duties. I learned there were three operating rooms, but each would have two to three simultaneous surgeries to accommodate all the patients. Such sharing of space would never be allowed in the United States due to infection control precautions, but here we had no choice.

Since it was Sunday and we couldn't yet begin working at the hospital, I was happy to accept an invitation from Dr. Weiss and Mike to join them on a half-hour drive by taxi to visit the Santa Barbara mine for a self-guided tour. The mercury mine has been closed since 1976, and the area has become a ghost town. A mercury miner's life expectancy was up to three years after he started working in the mine. Thousands of people died here because of the mercury exploited in the area.

Upon our return, I went to the market in the town plaza to purchase a hand-woven wool cap on display beside the commonly worn traditional bowler hats. Everywhere around the square, local merchants were selling hats, gloves, and scarves made from alpaca wool. The women, I soon discovered, each wore three layered, handmade skirts, called *polleras*, in lively patterns and brilliant shades. The majority of the women were rotund, with large breasts and tummies. I was told that their obesity issues were often related to their caloric intake from corn beer, or *chicha*, which locals commonly drank to stay warm. Everyone was friendly and appeared to be hardworking.

That evening, the staff of the local mining company presented us with a big dinner to welcome us and show their appreciation for our help, and they gifted each of us with a beautifully made hand-woven scarf. Throughout my stay, I ate potatoes and string beans. Many of my covolunteers dined on the local delicacy of guinea pig, which they claim tastes similar to the dark meat of chicken or duck.

The next day we awoke and gathered early, eager to start our work. As we arrived at the hospital, we found it was bustling with patients and staff. We went to greet the hospital director and thank him for making arrangements for us to work in his hospital. He was a very polite middle-aged man, and as I met his gaze I could clearly see he was afflicted with pterygium. The progressive condition of skin growing on top of the cornea is most common in environments where there is extreme dryness, heat, sun, wind, and cold. With a gentle smile I pointed out the condition, and he simply smiled back and acknowledged, "I'm aware of it."

Pterygium can not only irritate the eyes but also affect vision. As I began to evaluate patients, I found that about 80 percent of them were suffering with pterygium. I gave them anti-inflammatory drops and told the director to make the local ophthalmologist aware of the prevalence of pterygium so he could bring mytomycin C drops and Tisseel glue for amniotic membrane grafting with him on his next visit.

As the patients filed in, they and the staff began calling me Mamma Aisha. Perhaps they felt a kinship with me because, like them, I am short and brown-skinned. Several times I caught the women staring at my arms, and the interpreter informed me they were quite curious about my thin frame.

Although I saw more than 150 patients, throughout my stay I performed just three surgeries on the most urgent cases, with Dr. Kuon performing vascular surgeries just steps away from me. One of my cases was a thirty-year-old man who had traumatic light perception (written in the medical record as LP) cataracts. The other two cases were children, ages fifteen and five, both with eye lesions. The younger boy's mother had traveled more than one thousand miles for help, and fortunately I was able to remove the lesion completely, even though a local ophthalmologist was not on hand for follow-up care. Little Luis was so grateful about his recovery that he told me, through an interpreter, he wanted to bring me a baby parrot to take back to America. When I told him that the customs officials would not allow me to bring one back with me, he looked crestfallen, but he returned the next day with a wooden carving of a parrot, which I gratefully accepted.

There was no warm water in the OR and no way that I could withstand pouring ice-cold water over my hands for the standard five-minute surgical hand-washing. Instead, I soaked my hands with alcohol to sterilize them. The only antibiotic eye drops available in the hospital or the nearby pharmacy were chloramphenicol. The medication has been banned in the United States since 1978 because prolonged administration can cause aplastic anemia, a potentially fatal disease. Yet in developing countries, chloramphenicol is cheap and readily available.

After we'd spent a week in Huancavelica, the staff warmly thanked us, gave us certificates of appreciation, and escorted us to the door, where they all waved goodbye. After the arduous bus ride back to Lima, I said farewell to my fellow travelers and boarded a one-hour flight to Cusco, eager to learn more about this fascinating ancient culture. Cusco is a major tourist destination famous for its pre-Columbian architecture and colonial buildings, and just fifty miles from there is Machu Picchu, sometimes called the lost city of the Incas.

I was also able to visit the Cathedral of Santo Domingo in Cusco, a grand Catholic church constructed over a one-hundred-year period, some five hundred years ago, following the conquest of the Incas by the Spaniards. The elaborate structure was heavily adorned with gold leaf and cedar woodcarvings. Its many statues and paintings reflected Biblical accounts—with local flair. For instance, at the center of a huge painting, Marcos Zapata's rendition of da Vinci's "The Last Supper," was a food platter featuring a roasted guinea pig!

"*Ama sua, ama llulla, ama quella*," (Don't steal, don't lie, don't be lazy). For hundreds of years, Incas lived by this credo and even made it their formal greeting. Now ingrained into Peruvians' culture, the credo reflects the fusion of ancient Inca civilization harmonizing with the teachings of Catholicism.

Dr. Mora aptly described our experience with our appreciative Peruvian patients as both heartwarming and heart wrenching. A month

I joined doctors, nurses, and medical students from across the United States for this medical mission to Peru. *Photo by Mike Larremore*

after we returned from Peru, I invited the entire mission team to a reunion at my home, which many were able to attend. Over a lunch of traditional Burmese cuisine, we reminisced about our trip. For many members of our group, this was their first medical mission. I wasn't surprised to hear from several aspiring physicians and dentists that they had fallen in love with the people of Huancavelica and that they hoped this would be the first of many such altruistic adventures.

29
Ghana

*There is no better way to thank God
for your sight than by giving a
helping hand to someone in the dark.*

—HELEN KELLER

My trip to Ghana in August 2012 came by way of Mongolia and Richard Porowski, a patient from my practice in Orange. A few years ago as I examined Richard's light blue eyes in my office, he told me that he was leaving his civil engineering profession because he and his wife were moving to Mongolia, one of the poorest countries in the world. They saw a tremendous need to lift people out of poverty and volunteered to fill that need in whatever capacity they could.

In May 2011, Richard sent me an e-mail from Mongolia reporting that he and his wife, Kathy, were teaching English and he was serving as director of the Language Education Institute in Mongolia International University. He also included pictures of them hiking in the mountains near their city of Ulaanbaatar. A number of their students, and the adults bringing them to the school, had visible eye problems, he wrote, and they could use my help.

I immediately wrote back, "I am coming," and set in motion plans to be gone from my practice in August 2012 for a two-week visit. My niece and sponsored daughter Salma wanted to add her skills as a dermatologist,

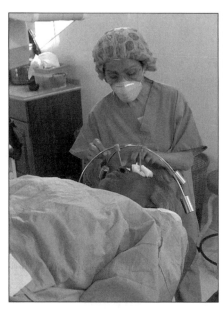

Prior to surgery at the clinic, this circular rod holds weights on the patient's eyes for several minutes so that the eyes are softened and the pressure within the eyeballs is reduced. *Photo courtesy of Aisha Simjee*

and a gastroenterologist colleague and her son also volunteered to go. Mike Larremore, a photographer from Denver, Colorado, whom I met on our 2011 mission trip to Peru, wrote me about a pulmonologist who wanted to join the trip. The doctor's research indicated that the Mongolian people had a high incidence of lung disease and death due to smog and pollution. A major cause of their respiratory illnesses can be traced to poorly ventilated homes, where stoves burn coal and garbage— including discarded rubber tires—throughout the harsh winters to keep residents warm.[1]

I was so pleased to have each of these volunteers joining me for the trip. Kathy personally talked with several influential people in the healthcare department of the area's teaching hospital as well as government officials about sanctioning our visit. But by May 2012, a year after initiating the project without making any headway and just over two months prior to our scheduled departure, with heavy hearts we had to abandon our plans.

Standing outside the Save the Nation's
Sight Clinic. *Photo courtesy of Aisha Simjee*

"I have not given up," I e-mailed Richard, urging him and Kathy to continue corresponding with local officials to support our offer of help. He wrote back that they would continue to work on the arrangements. Meanwhile, pediatrician Sudeep Kukreja, MD, from CHOC Children's Hospital in Orange County, invited me to go to Quito, Ecuador, along with several other members of CHOC's medical and nursing staff in February 2013, and I agreed to join them on the medical trip.

Since I had already set aside two weeks' time away from my office in August 2012, I contacted SEE International and asked for a recommendation of a place I could go and work where the need was most acute. Luis Perez, the international coordinator of SEE, had no problem suggesting a place and I had no problem accepting it, just as fast: Accra, in the Republic of Ghana.

Unfortunately, my would-be fellow travelers did not choose to accompany me to this remote West African country—for valid reasons. One concern that visitors to developing countries such as Ghana should take seriously is the high rate of communicable diseases. Whenever I travel to places with this problem, I take precautions to protect myself. I am careful about the sources of water I drink and bring protein bars for

At night, the clinic's waiting room becomes sleeping chambers for postop patients. *Photo by Aisha Simjee*

sustenance. I eat very little other food on these trips and return home healthy but a few pounds thinner.

Whether or not others travel with me is not something I can control. However, traveling solo definitely makes the trip more of a challenge, especially when it comes to hauling my equipment and supplies. I lugged four boxes to Ghana, and the airport had no ramps or escalators for passenger use. (On this trip, as was also true on my trip to Haiti, I was grateful to American Airlines for not charging me for my baggage. It was a welcome gesture, considering I had to pay Emirates Airlines $1,350 cash to bring supplies when I went to Afghanistan in May 2009.)

Accra, the country's bustling capital, is home to more than 2 million people. Fortunately, English is a fairly common language in Accra, although more than forty languages are spoken throughout Ghana. The former slave trading port on West Africa's Gulf of Guinea is today known as the gateway to Ghana. The country gained its independence from Great Britain in 1957. It has made recent strides in its economy and severe poverty level, but it has a long way to go. Many people still live in the poor shantytowns that have crept up around the fringes of the city and near the port. Limited access to clean water supplies and sanitation makes these people more vulnerable to diseases. They build cramped huts from sticks, palm fronds, plywood, discarded packaging, and any

I was welcomed by Dr. Thomas Tontie Baah (*second from left*), residents, and staff, who were eager to assist and learn eye care techniques. *Photo courtesy of Aisha Simjee*

other found materials. Barely surviving and feeding their families, they have no funds left to address debilitating medical and eye care issues that are often treatable.

In briefing me on the trip, SEE informed me that ophthalmology residents from neighboring Nigeria were driving to Accra to join the local Ghanaian residents and ophthalmologists and work with me. I immediately began preparing to give a talk on what is happening in anterior segment surgery in the United States and to exchange ideas on how they handled eye surgery with their limited resources.

I looked forward to meeting our hosting ophthalmologist, Dr. Thomas Tontie Baah, a dedicated foot soldier on the front line of Ghana's battle against preventable blindness. His medical calling began early; in childhood he lost his mother to measles and lived with his blind uncle. Today, he is one of Ghana's most respected eye care leaders.

Ten days before my visit, Ghana's president, John E. Atta Mills, died of throat cancer and the vice president, John Dramani Mahama, was quickly sworn into office. With cautious optimism, I read news reports of a stable transition.

I arrived in the heat of summer as the country's officials and dignitaries focused on an elaborate and lengthy funeral for Mills. News outlets reported hourly on the funeral plans and warned that major roads

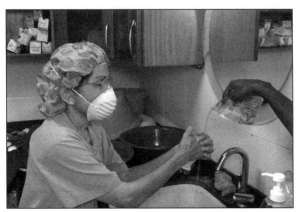

The operating room plumbing wasn't working while I was there. To sterilize my hands, staff poured precious clean water from bags. *Photo courtesy of Aisha Simjee*

throughout Accra would be blocked as thousands of mourners would pay their last respects to the departed leader. From the United States, Secretary of State Hillary Clinton attended the service. In light of the president's death, some of the local tourist destinations, including Osu Castle, where Mills would be buried, were closed for security reasons.

Although I did not voice my opinion at the time lest I offend someone, I found it ironic that in a place where current-day antibiotic eye drops were not available to the masses, within just a few days of the president's passing, the country had the wherewithal to post tributes, some as long as forty feet, all around town reading "Damirifa Due" (Rest in Peace). It seemed that every street corner had tribute banners along with vendors selling T-shirts, mugs, and trinkets imprinted with Mills's picture. There was no doubt that he was beloved by many Ghanaians.

Save the Nation's Sight Clinic, just a half-hour drive from the airport, was the private clinic where I worked most of the time. Ophthalmologists from several countries who had visited since it opened in 2009 had signed the clinic's guest book. The clinic is run by Dr. Baah and his wife, Charity Jaratu Issifu. Patients who lived in outlying areas arrived by way of the clinic's twelve-passenger buses and were taken home the day after their procedures. The nominal fee for their care was based on the area from which they came. Approximately one-third of patients from the villages had Ghanaian health insurance, and their eye surgeries were covered by the local health insurance system. Procedures for uninsured patients needing immediate surgical care were funded by the nonprofit global health delivery organization Unite for Sight.

I soon came to think of Dr. Baah as one of the hardest-working people I have encountered. Soft-spoken, serious, and small in stature, he hails from a tribe in northern Ghana. Like most of his countrymen, he has very dark skin. His face bears tribal marks: three linear scars on each cheek and one on his forehead. Scarification is an ancient practice that is performed by some of Ghana's northern tribes on their infants using a heated branding rod.

During the first seventeen years of Dr. Baah's medical career, he served as a family practitioner and obstetrician. He told me, "I delivered babies and performed C-sections in the mornings and would go to an eye clinic in the afternoons to do cataract surgeries." With very few to care for his countrymen's eyes, Dr. Baah felt obliged to do so, and now he dedicates all his time to their ophthalmological care.

The two-story Save the Nation's Sight Clinic included a reception area and waiting room, an examination room, a pharmacy, an optical shop, and an operating room. The OR, about the size of a one-car garage, contained three operating tables, microscopes, and a cabinet with surgical supplies. A sterilization canister on the clinic's patio was operated by a generator. At closing time, the waiting room was converted into a sleeping area with thin mattresses. The room accommodated postop patients brought from outlying villages who were without transportation to go home and return for postop checks the following day. Living quarters for Dr. Baah, his wife, son, and daughter were on the second floor of the building, next to the operating room.

When I told Dr. Baah I was impressed by his dedication, he simply smiled and said, "I am doing what I must do." At any hour of the day or night when a patient knocked on his door for emergency eye care, he would come out and attend to the person without complaint.

I went to work on patients presenting with advanced stages of glaucoma, cataracts, pterygium, and lid abscesses. I performed surgeries to remove both age-related and trauma-induced cataracts. The cataracts were either black and rock-hard, called *cataracta nigrecan*, or white and soft. Both types are indicative of very advanced stages, when it is difficult to predict a normal outcome after treatment. In Ghana, bilateral cataracts are frequently if not routinely operated on in the same sitting.

A few days after my arrival, Tissue Banks International in Baltimore generously sent us five corneas via airmail. In the United States, these corneas are sold for $3,300 each. Dr. Baah had to spend six hours at the airport customs office to retrieve the cornea parcel, in spite of the documents I had verifying that these were all charity items and not intended for commercial use.

I had learned that intraocular lens implants can be imported to countries such as Ghana from India for only 1 percent of the price we must pay for lens implants made and sold in the United States. Therefore, the latest antibiotic eye drops and ointments that the country has a difficult time procuring are considered more valuable. In Ghana, as in many developing countries I have visited, I saw tetracycline and chloramphenicol eye drops used to treat eye infections. These substances have not been used for eye care in the United States for decades because research suggests they can cause aplastic anemia.

A tall young resident who came to observe and assist, Dr. Raymond Toseafa, drove an hour and a half south from a medical clinic where he was stationed. He impressed me with his knowledge and was a good assistant for the cornea transplant surgeries.

Due to some conflicts in the border area, it turned out that only one Nigerian senior resident was able to make the fifteen-hour bus ride to

I delighted in visiting with staff and the many children at the Save Our Nation's Sight Clinic—patients such as these, as well as neighbors' and staff members' children. *Photo courtesy of Aisha Simjee*

Accra while I was there. Chizoba U. Nweke, MD, was a highly motivated young woman with a lovely smile who asked us to call her Cheesy. She assisted me with most of the procedures, and we had lively discussions regarding the different cases before and after the surgeries.

I brought with me five amniotic membrane grafts in the largest size available, each costing about $950 and graciously donated by Bio-Tissue, Inc., of Florida. I used them for clinic patients with pterygium and other ocular surface diseases, and saved two unopened graft packages to take to Ghana's premier healthcare facility, Korle-Bu Teaching Hospital. This two-thousand-bed hospital, teeming with patients, is located just a few miles from the clinic. The head of the hospital's Eye Unit, Dr. Stephen Akafo, and his associates and residents received me enthusiastically for a demonstration of amniograft transplants.

Of the thirty-five or so surgeries I performed during my visit, the most unusual case I saw was a woman who had "kissing" (touching) pterygiums at the three o'clock and nine o'clock positions in each eye, plus a pterygium at the six o'clock position in her left eye, for a total of five pterygiums. The patient was from a remote part of Ghana. We estimated she was about sixty-five years old, although like many elderly Ghanaians, she didn't know her exact date of birth or age.

A few hours prior to my departure, Dr. Baah and I tended to an elderly man and a middle-aged woman who both had advanced glaucoma, known as absolute glaucoma. Each had an eye with no vision and severe pain from extremely high eye pressure that made the eye rock-hard. Both required evisceration, the surgical removal of the contents of the eye with the sclera, the outermost part of the eye, and eye muscles left intact. We performed the procedures in the clinic's hallway since the operating room had been cleaned up for scheduled intraocular cases. After returning to my office, I sent the clinic two prostheses to reconstruct the globes, thus preventing eye globe shrinkage.

Ghana has only fifty-five ophthalmologists for an estimated 24 million people (roughly one ophthalmologist for a half-million people) and very few eye care facilities.[2] Herbalists and chemical sellers provide a form of eye care, but some of their practices are harmful. I observed that most of the people I encountered in Accra had red eyes, which I suspected was caused by some sort of allergy or poor hygienic conditions. It was very noticeable to me because in my practice in the United States, I've seen that Africans typically have very white eyes, envied by people of other nationalities. Some local people treated the condition with a breast-feeding mother's milk, as I was treated as a child with trachoma; other patients told me they used a mother's urine, which I gently discouraged. I realized I couldn't change their culture, but I hoped they would heed my advice.

I found several similarities in eye care in the different countries where I have worked—especially between Ghana and India, where I was involved with strictly low- or no-income clinics run by an NPO/NGO. The clinics were fairly well organized with dedicated staff. Also similar were the low cost of intraocular implants and the busing of patients to and from the clinics. And all these patients were fed lunch and then operated on, unlike in the States, where no preop patient is allowed so much as a drink of water after midnight in preparation for surgery the next day. As strange as many of these clinics' practices seem to me, I must say I admire their ophthalmologists for doing the best they can with the resources they have.

In spite of Ghana's status as a developing country and the poverty visible everywhere one looked, the people I met were decidedly cheerful and happy. The hotel personnel and clinic staff were prone to singing along with and sometimes dancing to the African percussion music on their radios—even in the operating room.

I lodged at a hotel located a few hundred feet down the road from the clinic. The best thing about this two-story hotel, which is better described as a motel, was its close proximity to the clinic. Its drapes were beyond dusty, there was no clock in the room, and unless I asked I did not get clean towels or hot water. Although originally I was told I would pay $50 a night, upon my arrival I was informed the fee was $70 a night and the hotel's machine for credit card processing was "broken."

I felt the hotel was taking advantage of me and other travelers, but I resolved not to let what I considered to be dishonest practices affect my outlook. Already charged an unexpected $150 at the airport for a working visa, I didn't have enough cash with me to cover my expenses and had to wire my husband for more money, which I received through Western Union, with a hefty service charge. Before checking out of the hotel I went to see the manager. I told him, "I'm not a fool and I don't believe the credit card machine is broken. If it is broken, why not fix it? You need to let people know that cash is required to stay in your place since most people don't carry that much money with them." He solemnly nodded, but I suspected I was just wasting my time, reminded once again of my inability to change the culture.

After my week at the Save the Nation's Sight Clinic, Cheesy agreed to go with me to Kakum National Park, a dense tropical rainforest about a hundred miles from Accra and just north of Cape Coast. Single file, we carefully traversed a rope bridge suspended one hundred to several hundred feet above the forest canopy. Cheesy chose the shorter of two courses, but I set out on the longer one. The view was breathtaking, but I don't mind admitting that the canopy walk made us more than a little nervous.

As I flew back home via London, England, and then Chicago, Illinois, I had time to rest and reflect on my time in Ghana. My thoughts turned to my patients and Ghanaian colleagues, who were so grateful for my time. The unspoiled staff expressed their delight in the writing pens and other portable gifts I left with them, and I was happy to accept from Dr. Baah a banner of yellow, green, and red—the colors on Ghana's flag—with my name embroidered on it.

I recalled how a number of patients introduced themselves to me. They would tell me their usually long names and some would indicate if they were either Christian, the religion of the majority of Ghanaians, or Muslim. Their faith preferences made absolutely no difference to me. Having seen religions do a great deal of good as well as some harm, I'm content to focus solely on fixing eyes as the purpose for my existence.

As Ghana's late leader John Atta Mills wisely said, "As a people, our greatest achievements have come when we have lived up to the ideals that unite rather than divide us and have attached ourselves to a common sense purpose."[3]

30
Orange, California

*In ordinary life we hardly realize that
we receive a great deal more than
we give, and that it is only with
gratitude that life becomes rich.*

DIETRICH BONHOEFFER

The Sisters of St. Joseph of Orange trace their history back to 1650 in Le Puy, France. Inspired by biblical accounts of Joseph's selfless care of Mary and Jesus, the sisters' foremothers served God and neighbors by ministering to the poor, sick, and orphaned. In 1922, the sisters moved to Orange, California, and officially became known as the Sisters of St. Joseph of Orange, opening St. Joseph Hospital in 1929. Throughout much of the last century, the sisters acted as day-to-day administrators for several acute-care hospitals they planted throughout California, in west Texas, and in eastern New Mexico. St. Joseph Hospital, where I practice, remains its flagship hospital, and at 525 beds it is the largest community hospital in Orange County. The sisters' lives of faith, grace, and charity won my respect, and the hospital provides a collaborative and compassion-filled place to practice.

Through the years, I have been honored to treat many of the sisters and three of the general superiors. Mother M. Louis Bachand, born in 1893, presided over the sisters from 1939 to 1951, and when I met her, she was in her twilight years. Brad Geagley's book *A Compassionate Presence* about the Sisters of St. Joseph of Orange describes Mother Louis as a woman of ethereal dignity, a teacher par excellence, and in her years as general superior, a woman clearly in charge.[1] On one of my house calls to see the sisters, Mother Louis clasped my hands and told me, "Bless you, Dr. Simjee. Surely you will go to heaven for your work."

I half-jokingly responded, "I live and work in heaven at St. Joseph Hospital." She beamed, knowing it was sincere and high praise for the healing environment the sisters had nurtured.

The late Mother Mary Felix Montgomery, born in 1897, presided over the sisters from 1951 to 1963. When I knew her in her later years, she served as a gracious and cordial hostess to all who used the St. Joseph Center facilities. This dignified, rail-thin woman was the "keeper of the keys," perpetually carrying a giant key ring holding what appeared to be about fifty keys for the various rooms. They seemed to be a microcosm of some impressive doors she had opened in her lifetime. Mother Felix presided over the opening of several schools and the expansion of their medical facilities and gave communities greater access to medical care by opening two hospitals. At the same time, her role called her to protect the sisters from encroachments of popular culture so they could stay true to their traditions in a time of great societal change. She was one of the last sisters to wear the customary veil.

In the late 1970s, I collaborated on patient care with the late Sister Frances Dunn, a sprightly elderly woman with a shock of white hair. Although she never used the title "Mother," Sister Frances served as the general superior for four years. During her health ministry she acted as the administrator for four hospitals, including St. Joseph and adjacent CHOC Children's Hospital, and led as president of the Hospital Council of California. Sister Frances managed to rattle some of the public's notions of how sisters should conduct themselves when she marched with farmworkers in the Los Angeles area, picketing a supermarket.

During her tenure she championed social justice and never turned a blind eye to the needs of the poor or migrant workers.

Faced with the "graying" of the sisters and recognizing the growing need for housing and infirmary care for their increasing number of elderly, Sister Frances spearheaded the building of a retirement home for the sisters, Regina Residence, which neighbors St. Joseph Hospital. For three decades, I've had the privilege of providing vision care at the residence for many of these dearly loved women who have given so much of themselves for the common good.

Sister Frances and another sister had been awarded the Walker Fellowship, given to healthcare executives to study hospitals and healthcare around the world. She and another sister spent about two months visiting Norway, Sweden, Italy, Pakistan, and India in the late 1960s. In the late 1980s, as she was entering her eighties and last decade of life, I would visit her at Regina Residence. Our conversations often turned to the medically underserved nearby and on the other side of our world. I would confide, "I really want to use my medical skills to bring dignity to poor people in countries where there seems to be little or no hope."

"Go," she would encourage me. "The need is so great and you could make such a difference!" She was certainly an inspiration to me, and after I began heeding my calling to make surgical expeditions, she was always eager to hear about my travels.

One of the sisters whom I thoroughly enjoyed treating came to me in her eighties for cataract surgery. This petite Caucasian woman with a pleasant, wrinkled face (who shall remain unnamed) was one of the last to wear the long, black-and-white habit. Not long after her successful surgery, I received a call from David Furnas, MD, a plastic surgeon and fellow staff member at St. Joseph Hospital who has since retired. I knew Dr. Furnas to be a very serious board-certified physician. So I was surprised when he demanded to know, with a hint of laughter in his voice, "What are you doing, Aisha? After you removed Sister's cataracts, she found she didn't like the way she looked and has come to me for a facelift!"

"I'm only doing my job," I defended myself. It never fails to makes me smile to remember this dear sister.

Sister Charleen Robinson was the first nurse administrator of Regina Residence. I've known her to be a kindly nurse and teacher for more than thirty years. She came to me in 2010 with severe uveitis, an inflammation of the uvea, the colored tissue of the eye. While she is fair skinned with blue eyes, this somewhat rare condition is more common in darkly pigmented races. In most cases, steroid drops are effective in relieving uveitis. Unfortunately, they did not work for Sister Charleen in spite of the fact that she is a registered nurse and an intelligent patient who fully complied with the prescribed treatment.

The drops promoted herpes simplex keratitis. It's a painful inflammation of the cornea that causes hazy vision, photophobia (sensitivity to bright light), redness, and tearing. Her condition rapidly advanced, resulting in a large ulcer in the cornea. A second opinion with one of my ophthalmologist colleagues confirmed my findings. Not accepting my feelings of helplessness concerning Sister Charlene's vision, I consulted by phone with an ophthalmologist in Miami on a treatment involving an amniotic membrane transplant. The amniotic membrane, obtained from fetuses in Cesarean deliveries, is grafted to the ocular surface. Amniotic membrane-covered surfaces induce rapid regrowth of a smooth, wet surface and reduce inflammation and scarring. When we discussed her having the procedure, Sister Charleen was hopeful. In our encounters she has never tried to proselytize, but she did tell me with conviction in her perpetually hoarse voice, "I believe in medical miracles. God can use scientific advances and medical technology to heal."

Sister Charleen asked her friends to pray for healing and did have a successful procedure, with functional vision restored. However, her chances for complete vision recovery are poor. Sometimes I am not able to cure my patients the way I would want. In all my surgeries and patient care management, I feel as if half of what is achieved is by my work, and the other half is in the hands of a higher power.

Another beloved sister who has been my patient for more than three decades, Sister Madeleva Williams, CSJ (Congregation of St. Joseph), has been a prolific artist during her more than sixty years in the religious order. Her paintings featuring quotations of faith, peace, and compassion adorn the walls of hospitals and homes and provide encouragement via greeting cards and bookmarks. "Beauty surrounds us," Sister Madeleva contends. "The trick is to recognize it."

Unfortunately, a few years ago Sister Madeleva was afflicted with age-related macular degeneration (ARMD) and she is now legally blind. When I first diagnosed her condition, I immediately referred her to a retina specialist for treatment to retain some useful vision, which she has been able to do.

ARMD is the leading cause of legal blindness in older adults via gradual destruction of the macula, the portion of the eye that provides sharp, central vision needed to view objects clearly. There are two types of macular degeneration: dry, which constitutes about 90 percent of ARMD cases, and wet, which affects Sister Madeleva. Neither is curable, but therapies can be provided to slow or stop the progression of wet ARMD. In developing countries, the condition is less common because of lower life expectancies, and the intensive treatment is much less likely to be available.

While still a presence in hospital operations and initiatives, the sisters' numbers have declined locally and beyond, in large part as a result of the emancipation of women. In past eras, a woman's "respectable" choices were to marry and have children or to join a religious order, but today we have limitless opportunities for service to others.

The St. Joseph Hospital Foundation is helping ensure that the sisters' ministry and legacy endure. Even though all the members of the foundation board do not share the Roman Catholic faith, they believe in the sisters' mission and in preserving the culture they established. I enthusiastically served on the foundation's board of directors for ten years, from 2000 to 2010. While I served on the board two of my grateful cataract patients donated several hundred thousand dollars to the foundation's nonprofit healing mission.

One of the ministries of the sisters called Bethany provides shelter and training to empower women who, due to domestic violence or other situations, find themselves homeless. It has been my pleasure to see some of these women from Bethany, whom I have treated for various eye conditions, go on to productive lives. One was Lisa Fallon, who took shelter at Bethany in 2002 to escape domestic violence.

During her transitional stay at Bethany's residence, I treated Lisa for a vision problem called lattice degeneration, a disease affecting the peripheral retina that can lead to a retinal tear and detachment and thus vision deterioration. "I didn't realize I was getting into an abusive relationship, but six months after I was married, I knew that if I wanted to live I would have to leave," Lisa later shared with me.

Since then she has healed, both physically and emotionally. I continue to monitor her eye health, and she's always smiling when she comes over to say hello as I run into the hospital cafeteria, where she works. It warmed my heart to hear her share recently, "Bethany helped me get on my feet again by helping me with budgeting and life skills. They helped me find a job and conquer my fears."

La Amistad De Jose, another ministry of the sisters and St. Joseph Hospital of Orange, helps the poor and disadvantaged in central Orange County with their health challenges. The clinic moved from Santa Ana to Orange several years back, and La Amistad is now just a three-minute walk from my office. La Amistad logs fourteen thousand visitors per year, from which I receive regular requests for voluntary ophthalmology consults. I don't ask about the patients' immigration status. Even if they are green-card eligible, these patients don't have the resources to take care of debilitating health issues. My view is that by restoring eye health, we can prevent a further drain on society by nurturing patients' current and future productivity.

Nine out of ten of La Amistad's patients speak Spanish. I can convey basic eye-related communication in Spanish and rely on bilingual staff in my office and at La Amistad. Most often the patients present with diabetes retinopathy, pterygium, glaucoma, and keratoconjunctivitis (inflammation of the cornea and conjunctiva), for which I prescribe medications they can get through the clinic.

While most find relief from their conditions, some of these children and adults require resource-intensive surgeries to alleviate their suffering. St. Joseph Hospital and Access OC, a nonprofit addressing specialty care needs of the uninsured population within Orange County, have orchestrated several free surgery days. Each has required approximately two hundred healthcare professionals, including about fourteen surgeons and me, volunteering on a Saturday. Assistant director of the St. Joseph Hospital Surgery Center, Diana Zirschky, RN, describes it this way: "Giving the person who has been waiting for ten years to have surgery but couldn't afford the intervention they needed and seeing gratitude on their face is such a great sacred encounter."

In 2010, St. Joseph Hospital's Emergency Department still included CHOC Children's Hospital emergency care and had California's second highest volume of emergency patients. I'm regularly called into the emergency room to help with some challenging cases. Two days after Christmas that year, a three-year-old Mexican boy arrived in the hospital's Emergency Department with a bite from the family pit bull. Multiple lacerations on the left side of his face included damage to his upper and lower eyelid. Luckily, the eyeball was not injured. I spent several hours repairing the lids, along with plastic surgeon Linda Zeineh, MD. The hospital social worker was required to report the attack to police. When I visited the toddler in CHOC he asked me, "When can I see my dog?" The dog had been euthanized, and I told the boy as gently as I could, "Your dog is gone because he hurt you, and we need to keep you and your family safe." I've seen the child several times since then, and he has recovered remarkably well, with minimal scarring and good vision.

That spring I also treated a sixteen-year-old Hispanic boy who was shot while walking down the street in Santa Ana, California. According to him, he was headed to the grocery store when an eighteen-year-old young man came by and shot him nine times. Bullets pierced the boy's arms and legs, one lodged in his thorax, and another one went through his left eyeball, completing rupturing the globe. His eye had to be removed so he would not contract traumatic sympathetic ophthalmia, which in certain cases results in vision loss in the uninjured, fellow eye. Through a hospital interpreter, his mother asked, "When will my son regain his sight in his injured eye?"

I replied, "I'm sorry, but the eye has been removed, and with the glass eye we placed in him, vision restoration will not be possible." Her frown told me she wasn't happy with my response, but it was the best I could do.

A few months later, a distraught child and his single Hispanic, probably undocumented, mother came to the ER. He had fallen down in their backyard exactly when a water sprinkler popped out, and it ruptured his globe. I performed the primary repair of the globe, but his vision will be very poor in that eye. He would need a cornea transplant to restore his eyesight. Expenses would be in the tens of thousands of dollars for medical supplies, utilization of medical facilities, and an operating room team, not to mention lifetime follow-up by me as his surgeon. All that I can do is gingerly follow his condition.

While many opportunities exist in my own backyard to care for medically underserved people, challenges arise from the legal ramifications. Unlike most foreign mission work, once I touch a patient in the United States. I am thereafter fully responsible for everything that can be done. These patients and their families often have high expectations but zero funds or insurance.

The Illumination Foundation, a nonprofit organization serving the homeless in Orange County, has contacted me a few times a year in the past decade to request my help with basic eye exams in the surrounding area. At the foundation's request, local ophthalmologist Keith Rundle, MD, an ophthalmic technician named Dixie, and I went to examine men and women seeking shelter at the armory in Santa Ana on a Saturday night in February 2011.

Dr. Rundle is strong and fairly young, which was helpful when he had to hold one woman while I examined her. A drug addict, she could barely sit up or keep her eyes open. Tattoos covered her neck, arms, and legs. Her eyebrows, nose, and lips were pierced and adorned with orange beads. She was one of the scarier-looking females I have ever treated, but at least her eyes didn't have any serious medical issues.

Another of the more than a hundred patients lying on armory mats was a fifty-year-old man who reeked of body odor and whose clothes were beyond filthy. He was balding and had a large bandage on the left side of his face that pulled down his lower eyelid and left him unable to fully blink (induced ectropion). As I examined him, I asked, "How did you get this injury?"

"Someone smacked me," he answered.

"Who did it?" I asked absently as I bent over him, but his response got my attention.

"That's a stupid question. If I knew, that guy would be dead by now," he snapped.

His answer revealed the typical mind-set of a street person. I was appalled not by his rudeness, but to see him amidst the milling throng of destitute people, spending the night just a few short miles from mansions housing some of the world's wealthiest citizens. In fact, affluent Orange County has one of the highest rates of homeless people per capita in the nation, as told to me by Orange County public health officer Eric Handler, MD, MPH.[2] I'm not a religious person, but as I left the armory, I prayed to the higher power, *Thank you for how well I am living, and please help me to help them.*

I have many interesting patients in my ophthalmic practice. One 101-year-old gentleman who came to see me left quite upset because I refused to sign his limited-mileage driving permit beyond six months, when he wanted it renewed for five years. This patient is consistently neatly groomed, often wearing a necktie and always with well-polished shoes. He doesn't have a single extra pound on his frame, and he walks straight and tall without the aid of a walker or cane. "I could drive blindfolded back and forth between the grocery store and my house," he insisted. While I admire his longevity and independent spirit, common sense prevailed.

In 2009 I performed surgery on a 101-year-old woman. In her day, she had been a beauty queen. She came in a wheelchair pushed by her great-grandson and wore pink lipstick, a pretty dress, and two-tone brown high-heel shoes. Before requiring a wheelchair, she had needed to wear orthopedic walking shoes, which she considered ugly. She told me cheerily, "Now that I'm in a wheelchair, I can enjoy wearing high-heel shoes without falling down!"

My patients have come from all walks of life, and I've learned from them all. From patients like this dear woman I'm reminded to look at the glass as half full. She teaches that how we look at life makes all the difference.

Aside from charity work, in my practice I see about 150 patients per week and perform at least 50 outpatient surgeries for cataracts and other conditions. I do various other vision consults and procedures for newborns, centenarians, and all patients in between. Young ophthalmologists periodically contact my office and ask if I have any plans to sell my practice. I invariably tell them, "Leave your name and number with my office staff so that if I drop dead, the staff can contact you to come and take care of the patients." I have no intention of retiring. Someday I may need to transition from surgical to medical ophthalmology if my eyes or hands fail me, but I plan to continue as an ophthalmologist as long as I am physically able.

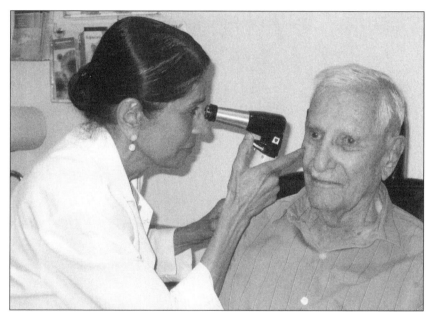

Barkev Baghdikian is an Armenian immigrant thriving in the United States. When he visited my office in 2012, he was 104 years of age. *Photo courtesy of Aisha Simjee*

Epilogue

America is too great for small dreams.
RONALD REAGAN

While compensation for my work is a right, recognition is a gift. Through the years I have received numerous gifts, including being named Physician of the Year in 2010 by the Orange County Medical Association (OCMA).

At the OCMA banquet, I felt especially gratified to be recognized by peers, my fellow physicians. I took the opportunity to thank them, as well as share these thoughts:

> Just as poor nations are plagued with a culture of corruption perpetuated from generation to generation, we in the United States are perpetuating our own cultural disgrace: a culture of waste. While many of the people I have encountered struggle to have one meal a day, the US Department of Agriculture reports that more than 25 percent of our country's food gets thrown in the garbage can. Did you know that if just 5 percent of Americans' food scraps were recovered it would represent one day's worth of food for 4 million people? Not to mention what we would save monetarily and environmentally without

the millions of tons of food waste that we as Americans
have come to accept as "normal."

Traveling throughout the world for the past six decades has made
me acutely aware of the disturbing culture of waste I see all around
me nearly every day here in America. A teenage girl whom I hired as
a file clerk in my office typifies this behavior. One day while at work, I
brought her a chicken salad sandwich. At the end of the day, I noticed
the entire sandwich had been thrown in the trash. "Didn't you like your
sandwich?" I gently asked.

"The bread looked soggy," was her nonchalant reply.

"Next time, perhaps you could take it home and toast the bread.
Then you or someone else in your family might be able to enjoy it," I
suggested. It made me sad and a little angry to see such waste. I know
that there are starving children in many parts of the world. This is not
a cliché to me—I have seen this sad reality.

I tell my own family not to become complacent about wasting food,
instructing, "If you are at a restaurant or party, take home what you
can't eat and give it to someone else, or have it the next day. When
taking food, get a small amount and if you are still hungry, then go
back for more. If it's put in front of you, ask the server to bring a box
and take it home."

As an active member of the Orange County Medical Association I
have attended countless delicious dinners. While I don't eat much and
rarely eat meat, I have no problem asking for a "doggie bag" to take
home to my husband. This habit initially raised some eyebrows among
the other physicians in attendance, but after a few dinners I noticed
that several other doctors began leaving with their leftovers as well.

On several occasions I have taken a day off work and paid my
own way to spend the day in Sacramento with the Orange County
Medical Association Legislative Committee. We are given a list

of assemblypersons and usually senators to speak to on a range of healthcare issues affecting patient care, the medical profession, and community well-being.

A few years ago, I met with a senator and told him what I saw when I was in Africa. "Bill Gates has donated $150 million for a vaccination program for children in South Africa," I said, "yet our local government can't give children in California vaccinations. They're not getting them through welfare, and many have no health insurance. The children are better off living in Africa. How do you justify that children in Orange County are not vaccinated?"

He looked at me, shrugged, and said, "This is politics." I stood up, bowed as I would have done in Burma to show my respect, and left. Perhaps if more people take up this cause, we will one day be successful in protecting all our children. Giving vaccines to select persons is not enough because diseases will be passed on. As an example, since 2010 several children have died while the United States deals with an epidemic of whooping cough due to inadequate vaccination rates.

How will our nation's current healthcare system evolve? I see a two-tier system coming. While I believe everyone deserves basic health services, it's also my opinion that people who work hard and have the means to pay for a higher tier of medical services of their choosing should have the right to do so.

I am not an easy person to impress, but I do have a great appreciation for honest people who work hard to better themselves and society. In 2005, I was invited to the annual UCI White Coat Ceremony, an event that marks the beginning of medical training for first-year medical students with the presentation of a white coat worn by medical professionals. That evening, I met the associate dean of admissions and outreach, Professor Ellena Peterson, PhD. As we have subsequently served together on the UCI Admissions Committee, which she chairs, I've come to know and admire Dr. Peterson.

Dr. Peterson has prevailed after twelve surgeries for head and neck cancer, beginning in 1993, and thirty-five radiation treatment sessions. Her voice has been ravaged by her condition and treatment, but she does not let the difficulty in speaking deter her. Not only is Dr. Peterson healthy and fit after overcoming a potentially fatal medical problem, but she is also one of the hardest workers I have ever met. She often works twelve hours a day, six days a week. I once asked about the source of her strength, and in her gravelly but firm voice she declared, "I have a strong will to survive."

After having lived in America for two-thirds of my life, I still wake up every day grateful to be a citizen, thriving with my family in this "land of opportunity." Each night I fall into bed spent and satisfied in my calling. I am blessed that there is always food on the table and a roof over my head and contented with a car that takes me where I need to go—with its odometer showing well over two hundred thousand miles.

I love America. I am living proof that this is a place where determined drive achieves goals and uplifts others in the process. Even seemingly outlandish dreams do come true.

Appendix

Charities Worthy of Support

Aloha Medical Mission
(808) 847-3400
http://www.alohamedicalmission.org
E-mail: info@alohamedicalmission.org

Armenian EyeCare Project
(949) 675-5611
http://www.eyecareproject.com

Arpan Global Charities (AGC)
(949) 757-4644
(714) 585-1920
http://www.arpanglobal.org
E-mail: arpanglobal@gmail.com

CHOC Children's
(714) 509-8690
http://www.choc.org

**Comprehensive Disaster Response Services (CDRS)
and SHINE Humanity**
(714) 665-2400
http://www.shinehumanity.org/index.php/getinvolved
E-mail: info@shinehumanity.org

Foundation of Goodness, Rainbow Clinic
(+94) (11) 2586344-5
http://www.unconditionalcompassion.org
E-mail: kushil@foquc.org

Hope *Worldwide*
(610) 254-8800
http://www.hopeww.org
E-mail: hope.worldwide@hopeww.org

Illumination Foundation
http://ifhomeless.org
(949) 273-0555

ORBIS International
(800) ORBIS-US
(800) 672-4787
info@orbis.org
http://www.orbis.org

St. Joseph Hospital Foundation
(714) 347-7900
(800) 887-8211
http://www.sjo.org/For-Community/Ways-to-Give.aspx
E-mail: foundation@stjoe.org

Surgical Eye Expeditions (SEE) International
(805) 963-3303
http://www.seeintl.org

Notes

Preface

1. "Visual Impairment and Blindness," World Health Organization, October 2011, http://www.who.int/mediacentre /factsheets/fs282/en/.

2. "Facts About Cataract," National Eye Institute, last reviewed September 2009, http://www.nei.nih.gov/health/cataract/cataract _facts.asp.

3. Ibid.

4. World Health Organization and International Agency for the Prevention of Blindness, *Vision 2020: The Right to Sight* (Geneva: WHO, 2007), http://www.who.int/blindness/Vision2020_report.pdf.

Chapter One: Burma

1. "Advances in Vision Science," National Eye Institute, National Institutes of Health, June 2011, http://www.nei.nih.gov/news /scienceadvances/discovery/trachoma.asp.

2. "Seventh July Student Massacre," Burma Digest, July 2, 2006, http://burmadigest.wordpress.com/2006/07/02/seventh-july-student -massacre/.

3. "Burma—Tuberculosis," Global Health Access Program, http:// www.ghap.org/programs/tb.

Chapter Two: America

1. Asif Siddiqi, "Pan American: The History of America's 'Chosen Instrument' for Overseas Air Transport," US Centennial of Flight

Commission, http://www.centennialofflight.gov/essay/Commercial
_Aviation/Pan_Am/Tran12.htm.

Chapter Three: Washington, DC, to California
    1. Elizabeth Fee, Theodore M. Brown, and Janet Laylor, "One Size
Does Not Fit All in the Transgender Community," *American Journal of
Public Health* 93, no. 6 (June 2003): 899–900, http://www.ncbi.nlm
.nih.gov/pmc/articles/PMC1447863/.

Chapter Four: Guyana
    1. To learn more, visit the SEE International website: http://www
.seeintl.org/aboutus/default.asp.

Chapter Six: Thailand
    1. Further information on ORBIS may be found on its website:
http://www.orbis.org/Default.aspx?cid=4830&lang=1.

Chapter Seven: Mexico
    1. For in-depth discovery of the Tarahumaras, I recommend
reading Bernard L. Fontana, *Tarahumara: Where Night Is the Day of
the Moon* (Tucson: University of Arizona Press, 1997).
    2. Cynthia Gorne, "A People Apart," *National Geographic*,
November 2008, 78–101, http://ngm.nationalgeographic
.com/2008/11/tarahumara-people/gorney-text/5; and Loera-Juan
Gonzalez, "Inequalities between Indigenous and Non-Indigenous
Populations in Northern Mexico" (master's dissertation, Institute of
Development Studies, 2008), 34–35, http://ids.academia.edu
/JuanLoera/Papers/909985/Inequalities_between_Indigenous_and
_Non-Indigenous_Populations_in_Northern_Mexico.

Chapter Nine: Republic of Georgia

1. More facts about this region can be found in "Georgia," *The World Factbook*, Central Intelligence Agency, updated October 21, 2011, https://www.cia.gov/library/publications/the-world-factbook/geos/gg.html.

Chapter Ten: Nigeria

1. For greater insights into the Nigerian dictator's reign and demise, see Mudiaga Ofuoko, "Abacha's Last Days" Online Nigeria, http://www.onlinenigeria.com/abacha_last_days.asp.

Chapter Eleven: Armenia

1. "Population of Armenia," Maps of the World.com, http://www.mapsofworld.com/armenia/armenia-population.html.

2. Michael Sheridan, "'Noah's Ark' Found atop Mount Ararat in Turkey, Evangelical Group Claims," NYDailyNews.com, April 27, 2010, http://articles.nydailynews.com/2010-04-27/news/27062831_1_mount-ararat-turkey-claims.

Chapter Twelve: Romania and Bulgaria

1. "1989: Romania's 'First Couple' Executed," BBC, December 25, 1989, http://news.bbc.co.uk/onthisday/hi/dates/stories/december/25/newsid_2542000/2542623.stm.

2. "Professor Petja Vassileva Elected to the AOI (Chair LXV)," *Academia Ophthalmologica Internationalis Newsletter* 12, no. 1 (2009), http://www.a-o-int.org/aoi-newsletter-2009.html#c88.

3. "Clinton Visits Bulgaria," PBS Online NewsHour, November 22, 1989, http://www.pbs.org/newshour/updates/november99/clinton_update_11-22.html; and John W. Handley, "Bulgarian Political Development 1989–2003," *American Diplomacy*, August

2003, http://www.unc.edu/depts/diplomat/archives_roll/2003_07-09
/handley_bulgaria/handley_bulgaria.html.

Chapter Thirteen: Bosnia

1. Laila Al-Marayati, "Violation of Human Rights against Women
in Bosnia-Herçegovina," Muslim Women's League, April 19, 1995,
http://www.mwlusa.org/topics/violence&harrassment/bosnian
_women.htm.

2. United Nations, "Empowerment of Women the Most Effective
Development Tool, Secretary-General Tells Commission on Status
of Women: Calls on International Community to Promote Gender
Equality and Invest in Women," press release, February 28, 2005,
http://www.un.org/News/Press/docs/2005/sgsm9738.doc.htm.

Chapter Fourteen: Philippines

1. Fely Marilyn E. Lorenzo et al., "Nurse Migration from a Source
Country Perspective: Philippine Country Case Study," *Health Services
Research* 42, no. 3 (June 2007): 1406–1418, http://www.ncbi.nlm.nih
.gov/pmc/articles/PMC1955369/.

2. "In Depth: Philippines," CBC News, updated March 10, 2008,
http://www.cbc.ca/news/background/philippines/index.html.

Chapter Sixteen: Nepal

1. B. Thylefors et al., "Available Data on Blindness," World Health
Organization, update 1994, 21, http://www.who.int/ncd/vision2020
_actionplan/documents/WHO_PBL_94.38.pdf.

2. Department of Economic and Social Affairs, *Rethinking
Poverty: United Nations Report on the World Social Situation* (New
York: United Nations, 2009), 26–27, http://www.un.org/esa/socdev
/rwss/docs/2010/fullreport.pdf.

3. "Nepal Self-Reliant in Eye Treatment," *Blind World Magazine*, January 16, 2006, http://home.earthlink.net/~blindworld/NEWS/6 -01-16-03.htm#TOP.

4. Kul Chandra Gautam, "Envisioning a New Nepal with Priority for Children" (lecture, B. P. Koirala Eye Foundation, Kathmandu, Nepal, April 2, 2010), http://bpeyefoundation.org/downloads /Publication/Kulchandra%20Gautams%20lecture%20on%20 disability%20-%20april%202010.pdf.

Chapter Seventeen: Afghanistan

1. Laura King, "Taliban Ambush Kills Aid Workers," *Los Angeles Times*, August 8, 2010.

2. Karen Woo, "Medical Expedition," Bridge Afghanistan (blog), August 7, 2010, http://bridgeafghanistan.blogspot.com/.

3. USAID/Afghanistan, "Frequently Asked Questions," http:// afghanistan.usaid.gov/en/about/frequently_asked_questions.

4. For more information on Hope *Worldwide*, visit http://www .hopeww.org.

5. World Health Organization and Afghan Red Crescent Society, "13 Million Afghans at Risk of Contracting Leishmaniasis, Says WHO," press release, October 14, 2010, http://www.who.int/hac /crises/afg/afghanistan_press_release_14oct2010.jpg.pdf.

Chapter Eighteen: Panama

1. Bureau of Western Hemisphere Affairs, "Background Note: Panama," US Department of State, http://www.state.gov/r/pa/ei /bgn/2030.htm.

2. Ibid.

Chapter Nineteen: Ethiopia

1. "Guide to Ethiopia," Link Ethiopia, http://www.linkethiopia
.org/guide/travellers/travel_tips/time.html.

Chapter Twenty: Sri Lanka

1. Preeti Bhattacharj, "Liberation Tigers of Tamil Eelam (aka
Tamil Tigers) (Sri Lanka, separatists)," Council on Foreign Relations,
updated May 20, 2009, http://www.cfr.org/terrorist-organizations
/liberation-tigers-tamil-eelam-aka-tamil-tigers-sri-lanka-separatists
/p9242.

2. Kate Pickert, "A Brief History of the Tamil Tigers," *Time*,
January 4, 2009, http://www.time.com/time/world/article
/0,8599,1869501,00.html.

Chapter Twenty-One: India

1. International Development Association, "IDA at Work, India:
Cataract Blindness Control Project," updated September 2008, http://
web.worldbank.org/WBSITE/EXTERNAL/EXTABOUTUS/IDA/0
,contentMDK:21917842~pagePK:51236175~piPK:437394~theSite
PK:73154,00.html.

2. Prasant Sarangi and Satyabrata Pattanaik, "Poverty and
Performance of Major Welfare Schemes in Gajapati District," *Orissa
Review*, May 2006, http://orissa.gov.in/e-magazine/Orissareview
/may2006/engpdf/37~44.pdf.

3. To read more about this remarkable eye care system, visit
http://www.aravind.org/vanakkam/homepage.aspx.

4. "2008 Gates Award for Global Health: Aravind," Bill & Melinda
Gates Foundation, http://www.gatesfoundation.org/gates-award
-global-health/Pages/2008-aravind-eye-care-system.aspx.

5. "Aravind to Receive $1.5 Million Hilton Humanitarian Prize," Conrad N. Hilton Foundation, March 5, 2010, http://www .hiltonfoundation.org/prize-aravind.

6. Bill & Melinda Gates Foundation, http://www.gatesfoundation .org/press-releases/pages/india-aravind-eye-care-award-080521.aspx.

Chapter Twenty-Two: Myanmar (Burma)

1. Rachel Harvey, "Is Burma's Political Landscape Changing for Good?" BBC News Asia, November 18, 2011, http://www.bbc.co.uk /news/world-asia-15790290.

2. "Myanmar Government Would Face Revolutionary Change If They Shun Evolutionary Reform—Senator McCain," *Yangon Press International*, June 2011, http://www.yangonpress.com/index.php /article/view/37/Myanmar+government+would+face+revolutionary +change+if+they+shun+evolutionary+reform+B+Senator+McCain.

3. "Yangon: From Stately City to Crumbling Symbol of Isolation," November 26, 2011, http://www.reuters.com/article/2011/11/27 /us-myanmar-yangon-idUSTRE7AQ02020111127.

Chapter Twenty-Three: Egypt

1. "Egypt-Religion," GlobalSecurity.org, http://www .globalsecurity.org/military/world/egypt/religion.htm.

2. "Trauma Grips Survivors of Church Blast in Alexandria," Compass Direct News, January 31, 2011, http://www.compassdirect .org/english/country/egypt/32050.

Chapter Twenty-Four: Colombia

1. To learn more about ARPAN, see http://www.arpanglobal.org/.

Chapter Twenty-Five: Cambodia

1. "Cambodia," *The World Factbook*, Central Intelligence Agency, updated November 9, 2011, https://www.cia.gov/library /publications/the-world-factbook/geos/cb.html.

2. A. R. Rutzen, "Blindness and Eye Disease in Cambodia," *Ophthalmic Epidemiology* 14, no. 6 (November–December 2007): 360–366; and Enitan Sogbesan, "Cambodia's National Eye Care Programme and VISION 2020: The Right to Sight," *Journal of Community Eye Health* 13, no. 36 (2000): 57–59, http://www .cehjournal.org/0953-6833/13/jceh_13_36_057.html.

3. "UNESCO Helps Preserve Tuol Sleng Genocide Museum Archives in Cambodia," September 10, 2009, http://portal.unesco .org/ci/en/ev.php-URL_ID=29102&URL_DO=DO_TOPIC&URL _SECTION=201.html.

4. "Choeung Ek, Center of Genocide Crimes," International Center for Transitional Justice, http://memoryandjustice.org/site /choeung-ek-center-of-genocide-crimes/.

5. "Cambodian Genocide Program," Yale University, http://www .yale.edu/cgp/.

Chapter Twenty-Six: Haiti

1. Martha Kerr, "AMA Urges Restraint for Clinicians Seeking to Volunteer in Haiti," USF Health, updated January 17, 2010, http:// hscweb3.hsc.usf.edu/health/now/?p=9971.

2. "Haiti Raises Earthquake Death Toll to 230,000," MSNBC, updated February 9, 2010, http://www.msnbc.msn.com/id/35319454 /ns/world_news-haiti/t/haiti-raises-earthquake-death-toll /#.TrhGV2B5FbU.

3. The following in-depth article is on Sean Penn's work in Haiti: Douglas Brinkley, "Welcome to Camp Penn," *Vanity Fair*, July 2010, 84–91, 141–143.

Chapter Twenty-Seven: Pakistan

1. "2011 UNHCR Country Operations Profile—Pakistan," United Nations High Commissioner for Refugees, http://www.unhcr.org /pages/49e487016.html.

2. Nahal Toosi, "Pakistan Flood Damage Estimated at $9.5 Billion," MSNBC, updated October 13, 2010, http://www.msnbc.msn .com/id/39657931/ns/world_news-south_and_central_asia/t/pakistan-flood-damage-estimated-billion/#.TrhRVmB5HfY.

3. "UN Chief Ban Ki-Moon: Pakistan Floods Are Worst Disaster I've Ever Seen," *Huffington Post*, updated May 25, 2011, http:// www.huffingtonpost.com/2010/08/15/pakistan-floods-ban-ki-moon_n_682649.html.

4. More about the work of SHINE Humanity can be found on its website: http://www.shinehumanity.org/.

Chapter Twenty-Eight: Peru

1. "Poverty Profile: Peru" Japan Bank for International Cooperation, October 2007, http://www.jica.go.jp/activities/issues /poverty/profile/pdf/peru_e.pdf.

2. Pan American Health Organization, http://www.paho.org /english/dd/ais/cp_604.htm.

Chapter Twenty-Nine: Ghana

1. Christa Hasenkopf, "Clearing the Air," *World Policy Journal*, Spring 2012, http://www.worldpolicy.org/journal/spring2012 /clearing-air.

2. "Global Optometry: Changing and Challenging, Non-Physician Providers—Lessons Learned Around the World," World Ophthalmology Leaders Forum in Education, 2011, http://www .aao.org/international/wolfe/upload/WOLFE_global_optomtery _forum_2011-3.pdf; and "2010 Population Census: Ghana Hits over

24m," GhanaWeb, May 31, 2012, http://www.ghanaweb.com /GhanaHomePage/NewsArchive/artikel.php?ID=240611.

3. Chris Twum, "GUBA's Tribute to Late President Atta Mills," *Ghanaian Chronicle*, August 31, 2012, http://ghanaian-chronicle.com /gubas-tribute-to-late-president-atta-mills.

Chapter Thirty: Orange, California

1. Brad Geagley, *A Compassionate Presence: The Story of the Sisters of St. Joseph of Orange* (Orange, CA: Sisters of St. Joseph of Orange, 1987).

2. Dr. Handler's assertion is confirmed in this study: "Homeless Counts in Major US Cities and Counties," United Way of Greater Los Angeles, December 2005, accessed November 6, 2011, http://www .unitedwayla.org/getinformed/rr/research/basic/Documents /2005HomelessCities.pdf.

Index

About the Author

Aisha Simjee, MD, is a board-certified and fellowship-trained ophthalmologist. She has served patients for more than thirty-five years in her Orange County, California, practice and through numerous charitable organizations. The Burma native and naturalized United States citizen has taken twenty-six medical mission trips to twenty-five countries in the past twenty-one years and plans to visit several more countries in the coming years. Because of her extraordinary services to help sightless and suffering people around the world, she has received the following awards:

- 1990 Annual Women of Achievement Award, Rancho Santiago Community College, Santa Ana, California

- Certificates of Recognition from the following officials:
  California State Senator John Seymour
  California Congressman Christopher Cox
  California Lieutenant Governor Leo McCarthy

- 1993 Values in Action Award for Service, St. Joseph Hospital

- 2004 Humanitarian Services Award, Orange County Board of Supervisors

- 2005 Pride in the Profession Award, American Medical Association

- 2006 Women of Vision Award, We Give Thanks

- 2010 Physician of the Year, Orange County Medical Association

- 2012 UCI School of Medicine Voluntary Faculty J. Edward Berk Physician Award for Humanitarian Services

Dr. Simjee continues to dedicate her life to helping visually impaired people—both at home and around the world.

CORE COLLECTION 2013